COLCHESTER
A History

ST-BOTOLPHS-PRIORY-ESSEX-

John Sell Cotman's view of the ruined west front of St Botolph's Abbey church captures the theme of ancient grandeur which has sustained Colchester's public identity for 200 years. Cotman's drawing sold in some numbers in 1836 to help fund the building of the present St Botolph's Church.

COLCHESTER
A History

Andrew Phillips

Phillimore

2004

Published by
PHILLIMORE & CO. LTD
Shopwyke Manor Barn, Chichester, West Sussex, England

© Andrew Phillips, 2004

ISBN 1 86077 304 4

Printed and bound in Great Britain by
CAMBRIDGE PRINTING

Contents

List of Illustrations

Frontispiece: St Botolph's Priory

Introduction
and Acknowledgements

❖

Few towns in Britain can match Colchester for the depth and drama of its history. In this book I hope ordinary readers will find not just headline-grabbers like Julius Caesar and Boudica, King John and Henry VIII, but the ordinary people of Colchester pursuing their often hazardous lives. I have also given full coverage to the 20th-century history of the town, the bit many readers will actually remember. A history book should always be a bridge to the future and not just a detour from the present.

In writing a concise history there are two challenges. Firstly, there is real difficulty in deciding what to leave out. Complex issues must often be reduced to a simple story. Secondly, I am heavily indebted to other writers who know more about certain periods than I do. In particular, I would like to thank Philip Crummy of the Colchester Archaeological Trust and author of *City of Victory*, for help with the early chapters and the use of illustrations from his books,

Reconstruction by the artist Peter Froste of Roman Colchester in *c*.A.D. 250. The Temple of Claudius can be seen in the north eastern sector.

Janet Cooper, editor of the outstanding *Victoria County History of Essex*, *Volume 9*, about Colchester, and Ian McMeekan, of the Colchester Tourist Guides, who have read individual chapters. Paul Sealey introduced me to 'British G' coins. I have suggested, in the Bibliography, books where an interested reader might find more detailed information.

Keith Mirams drew the cloth trade illustrations and Brian Light the map of Roman Britain, while the incomparable Peter Froste has kindly permitted me to include several of his historical paintings. The Colchester Museum Service were helpful in supplying a great many images. Marcel Glover digitalised other images. In addition, I would like to thank the following individuals, institutions and publications for the use of photographs and illustrations, for which they hold the copyright: Barracuda Books, Colchester Archaeological Trust, *Colchester Evening Gazette*, Colchester Museum Service, Essex County Council Archaeological Unit, Essex Society for Archaeology & History, John Byford, Tony London, Martin Simmons, David Stephenson, Jenny Stevens, Daphne Woodward.

Andrew Phillips
March 2004

One
Camulodunum
50 B.C.–A.D. 60

Colchester boasts 2,000 years of history. Even in England this is remarkable. Hence the tourist slogan that Colchester is 'Britain's Oldest Recorded Town.' Is this correct? In part that depends on what is meant by a 'town'. To see why, we must turn to the eye-witness account of these islands and their inhabitants provided by Julius Caesar. We can also learn from archaeology, whose evidence is frequently dramatic.

Although there had been settlements in what is now Essex for centuries before his arrival,

Julius Caesar's assault across the Channel in 55 B.C. provides our first documented history. By his own account Caesar was invading on the pretext that one British king had murdered another and his son, Mandubracius, had fled to Caesar for protection. Mandubracius was a prince of the Trinovantes, a tribe inhabiting most of modern Essex and South Suffolk. The Trinovantes were, Caesar wrote, 'about the strongest [tribe] in south-east Britain'.

Caesar's 55 B.C. invasion came close to total disaster. Hence his return in 54 B.C.

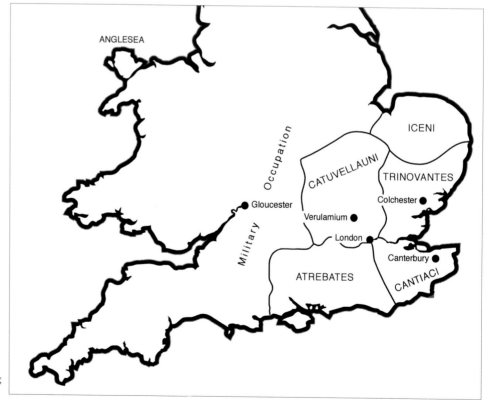

1 Roman Britain in c.A.D. 60, showing tribal divisions.

1

2 Four gold coins (staters) produced under Cunobelin bearing CAMU for Camulodunum and CUNO for Cunobelin.

with a larger army and an enormous navy. This time the Britons united under the leadership of Cassivellaunus, whose stronghold Caesar eventually attacked and overran. The

evidence suggests that Cassivellaunus was king of the Catuvellauni, a tribe based on modern Hertfordshire, the next-door neighbours of the Trinovantes and the alleged murderers of the father of Mandubracius. The Trinovantes now appealed to Caesar to install Mandubracius as their king and to protect him from Cassivellaunus. These two tribes, the Catuvellauni and the Trinovantes, apparently hold the key to the origin of Colchester.

Though Caesar had conquered no territory, he had, during his invasion, established direct links with several British tribes. Over the next 100 years, from its close trading contacts with Rome, the south-east became the power centre of Britain. This was a two-way process; not only did British grain, hides, metals and slaves reach the Roman world, but Roman luxuries were traded to the British aristocracy, spectacular evidence of which has been found in a series of royal or aristocratic graves,

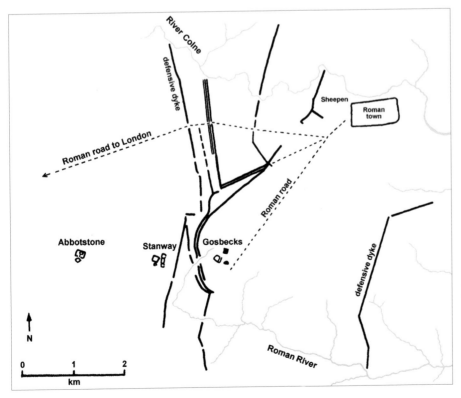

3 The dyke and river system which defended Camulodunum, showing the Iron-Age farm at Abbotstone, the burial site at Stanway and the Roman town which forms the core of modern Colchester.

4 Gryme's Dyke, today the western boundary of Colchester, still shows some of its rampart defences, despite 2,000 years of erosion.

many near Colchester. The distribution of a coin called 'British G', current around 50-25 B.C., suggests that Colchester was already an important centre. Significantly, very few 'British G' coins have been found to the west in Catuvellauni territory.

British kings now began to issue coins carrying their own names, often tied to a specific mint. In the absence of any written British language, the coins carry Latin script, further evidence of Roman influences. The first king to name a mint was Tasciovanus, king of the Catuvellauni, and presumably a descendant of Cassivellaunus. His mint was at Verulamium (now St Albans), the tribal 'capital', but early in his reign he also issued coins from Camulodunum (now Colchester), presumably in Trinovantian territory.

From about A.D. 5 Cunobelin, described as the 'son of Tasciovanus' (Shakespeare calls him Cymbeline), also began to issue coins from Camulodunum – and only Camulodunum – and issued them in great numbers for over thirty years: perhaps a million gold coins according to a recent estimate. We must conclude that the Catuvellauni royal family, or Cunobelin at least, had made Camulodunum their new power base. It is easy to see why the port access this provided to the Roman world might be preferable to land-locked Verulamium. How far this entailed conquering the Trinovantes we do not know.

Camulodunum was very large – about ten square miles – and well defended, flanked to the north and east by the River Colne, to the south by the Roman River. To the west a whole

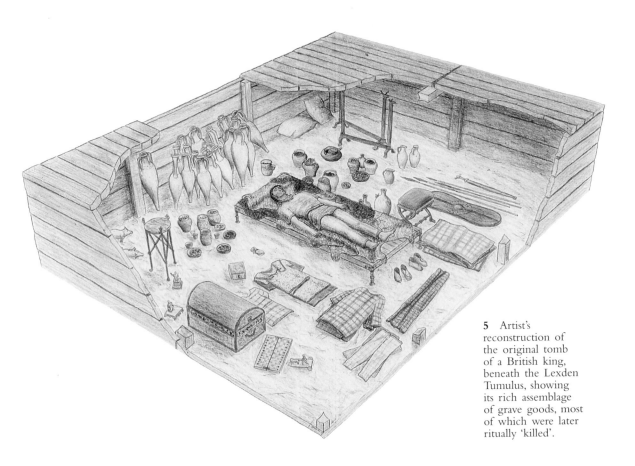

5 Artist's reconstruction of the original tomb of a British king, beneath the Lexden Tumulus, showing its rich assemblage of grave goods, most of which were later ritually 'killed'.

series of dykes was built (earthen ramps and ditches), clearly meant to be defensive against the chariot warfare at which the British were so adept. Added together the dykes stretched perhaps 12 miles, an enormous investment in labour, though it should be pointed out that a good deal of the system was built or extended after the Roman Conquest. The Romanised name of Cunobelin's stronghold – Camulodunum – is also significant. It means the fortress (dunum) of Camulos, the British war god. But was it a 'town'?

The Romans did not think so and described the larger British settlements as 'oppida' (strongholds), not 'urbes' (cities). This would be reinforced by Camulodunum's appearance. On present evidence much of it was rural, given over to fields and livestock, particularly cattle, and scattered settlements. Two areas of importance have been identified. At Sheepen, where shallow boats could be brought up the tidal River Colne, a manufacturing and commercial area existed. In particular, coin moulds have been found for Cunobelin's formidable output of currency.

Perhaps more interesting is the second area at Gosbecks, much of it now set aside as the Gosbecks Archaeological Park. This appears to have been based on a large farmhouse complex surrounded by a ditch, cattle trackways and fields. A 'sacred' area nearby was later to house a temple. It has been interpreted as a royal centre, presumably of Cunobelin himself. From here during his extraordinarily long reign, Cunobelin's trading network extended over much of southern England, where he held the status of a paramount king, termed by one Roman writer the 'king of the Britons'. Indeed, it was tribal conflicts following his death, in which his sons appear to have been aggressors, that provided the pretext for the Roman conquest of Britain, 98 years after Julius Caesar's first cross-Channel raid.

One other sign of Camulodunum's importance must be mentioned: the contents of several remarkable graves. The most significant is the Lexden Tumulus, a large burial mound (today in someone's back garden), datable to 15 to 10 B.C. and found to contain the richest collection of grave goods known for that date in Britain: at least 17 Roman amphora (wine flagons), rich garments, chain mail armour, a collection of figurines and vessels of copper. As part of the burial ritual most of these objects had been deliberately broken up. There may therefore have been more objects than we now have. The entire burial was probably placed within a large wooden chamber. Quite the most important find was a silver medallion of the Emperor Augustus, arguably presented to the buried man. On date evidence this could be Addedomarus, whose issue of Camulodunum coins ends about this time.

There are other burials. At Stanway several important chambered graves in ditched enclosures have been excavated, containing high status tableware, drinking vessels and other symbols of wealth, ritually broken up. Most significantly, as we shall see, most of these burials actually date from after the Roman Conquest.

The Roman Invasion

It had probably been Rome's intention to control Britain since the days of Julius Caesar. An invasion was finally launched in A.D. 43 by the Emperor Claudius. Significantly, a large Roman army made straight for Camulodunum. Landing in modern Kent, several bloody battles were fought, probably at the River Medway and near a crossing of the Thames. Here one

6 Two crucial finds in the Lexden Tumulus: (i) delicate silverwork of ears of corn, which recall the grain on the coinage (ii) a silver medallion of the Emperor Augustus, perhaps a personal gift from the Emperor.

of Cunobelin's sons, Togodumnus, was killed. Another son, Caratacus, lived to fight on and subsequently became an inspirational guerrilla fighter against the Roman advance, continuing the struggle in the Welsh hills.

Meanwhile, north of the Thames, the invading army halted until they were joined by the Emperor Claudius himself, bringing, a Roman historian tells us, additional equipment and war elephants. Such a long journey from Rome, the only one the Emperor ever took, in order to lead his troops against the British stronghold, tells us volumes about the importance of Camulodunum, even if the whole event was carefully stage-managed. In a stay of just 16 days, Claudius took Camulodunum and received the submission of a number of native kings. Back in Rome his achievement was considered sufficiently real for him to have two triumphal arches built, a 'triumph' parade held in Rome and the title Britannicus granted to his son.

With Camulodunum subdued, the Roman army continued its advance north and west. Within four years most of south-east Britain, so long in contact with the Roman world, was subdued. This was not solely the result of battle: Rome had long known how to divide

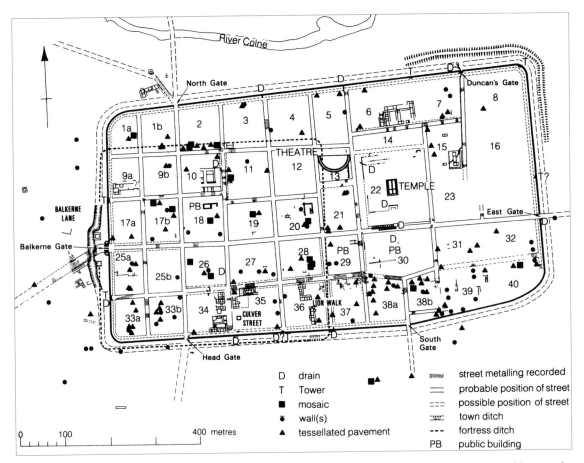

7 An archaeological plan of the Roman Colonia, showing the street grid, the known excavated buildings, and the ditch of the earlier fortress marked with a dotted line.

and rule. The invasion itself owed much to the friendly support of the Atrebates (in modern Sussex), who were now restructured as a client kingdom. Likewise the tribe to the north of the Trinovantes, the Iceni (modern Norfolk and part of Suffolk), were allowed to retain their autonomy under Prasutagus, a pro-Roman member of their royal family. It is a matter of some interest as to how the Trinovantes themselves were now treated.

In Caesar's day they had been pro-Roman, seeking his help against their neighbours the Catuvellauni. Yet those neighbours had established their 'capital' in Trinovantian territory. The great Cunobelin was a Catuvellauni king ruling from Camulodunum. His sons led the

fight against the Roman invasion. That was why the Emperor came to receive the surrender of Camulodunum. On whose side were the Trinovantes? We must assume they had accepted the rule of Cunobelin and his sons. Otherwise they deserved better from the Romans than what followed.

The XXth Legion, almost 5,000 strong, were to be housed in a permanent fortress built on a gravel ridge above the River Colne, a high point where today the town centre of Colchester stands. It commanded the heights above the Sheepen industrial area and stood uphill from the furthest point of tidal navigation. Built according to Roman military design, it was roughly four-square, 510 metres long, 445 metres wide, running west-east along the ridge, enclosing in all an area of some fifty acres, surrounded by a deep ditch and earth rampart. Inside were some sixty barrack blocks, the commander's headquarters, stores and other buildings. Nothing on this scale had been seen in Britain before, and the manpower, logistics and assembly of material that it called for would vividly demonstrate Rome's formidable administrative resources. Modern Colchester was thus Rome's first command and control base in Britain.

The conquest of Britain meanwhile made slow progress. Tribes resident in what is now Wales were harrying the Roman forces, assisted by the second son of Cunobelin, Caratacus, who became a legend for his exploits against the Romans. The new governor of Britain resolved to move the XXth Legion from Camulodunum to the vicinity of Gloucester. As they left, the new legionary fortress was re-designated a colony, the foremost type of Roman city. Manned by retired Roman soldiers, it would have had its own Imperial charter, public services and a city council, serving as an example of Roman civilisation to the native population. It was also, for the present, the capital of Britannia, the new province. On this basis Colchester can claim to be Britain's first town.

It was very much a planned town, its grid of intersecting streets varying only slightly from the layout of the legionary fortress. But the new colony did not consist solely of streets and buildings. It would have had its own 'territorium', land surrounding the town, divided into plots and farmed by the Roman citizens of the colony. Given a likely population for the built-up area of 2,000, the 'territorium' would have extended for several miles around. Such land may have been taken from estates owned by the Catuvellani royal family, but it seems also to have included Trinovantian territory.

8   A museum model, with figures for scale, of the Temple of Claudius, based on the known style and proportions of such a building.

This did not endear the Romans to them. Nor did the town's largest public building: a majestic classical temple dedicated to the Emperor Claudius, now declared a god, following his sudden death in A.D. 54. This, the largest classical temple known from Roman Britain, promoted the imperial cult of Emperor worship and of the goddess Roma. Financed by heavy taxation of the local population, there could be no clearer statement of Roman economic and cultural imperialism. There was also, according to the Roman historian Tacitus, a large statue dedicated to Victory, with the name of the new town reinforcing this message: Colonia Victricensis – Colony of the Victorious.

Remarkably, we can still see the base of the Temple of Claudius. One thousand years later a Norman castle was built on its foundations. Mortar poured by the Romans onto shuttered mounds of sand (since removed) now forms 'vaults' under that castle. The Temple was set in a large courtyard, apart from the rest of the town. Archaeology has shown that many of the buildings in the legionary fortress were

9   The temple foundations, once filled with sand, now form vaults under Colchester Castle.

adapted for re-use in the new town; indeed, with a slight realignment and an extended grid of streets, the Colonia was essentially an eastward extension of the fortress. This eastern end housed a number of public buildings, of which the Temple and a theatre soon existed. It is also possible that coins issued at this date from a mint in north-west Europe bearing the head of Claudius were minted here. Many have been found in the town.

Colonia Victricensis was, then, a distinct creation within the wider confines of Camulodunum: it had not become Camulodunum, and the old tribal capital was itself transformed. The Sheepen site extended its manufacturing capabilities, undertaking leather and metal working which probably involved the maintenance of Roman military equipment. The Gosbecks complex, the former royal farmstead two miles from Colonia Victricensis, with its sacred temple site, also appears to have remained British, but was overseen by the new rulers. The dyke system protecting the exposed western approach to Camulodunum was considerably strengthened and extended; some of this may have related to whatever military activity accompanied the Claudian conquest. A Roman road also linked the area with the new town, and a military fort, capable of housing 500 men, was built just inside the dykes which flanked the Gosbecks area.

If Gosbecks suggests some accommodation with continued British cultural traditions, an even more tantalising suggestion lies just outside its protective dykes in five enclosed graves excavated in recent years at Stanway, the earliest pre-dating A.D. 5. These enclosures contained chambered tombs with grave goods ritually broken up, such as we noted in the Lexden Tumulus. In some enclosures subsidiary graves appeared to house lesser members of the British aristocracy. One contained a doctor's surgical instruments, similar to the most advanced in the Roman world; another contained an inkwell, suggesting literacy; another contained a spear and a shield, implying the right to bear arms. Had the occupant perhaps served with the Roman army? These graves date to after the Conquest. Yet Cassius Dio, a Roman historian, clearly states that all the tribes who surrendered to Claudius were disarmed. Here, surely, we have evidence of a British regime continuing in some client relationship to the Romans, permitted to exercise a degree of their former power and traditions in return for keeping the system going, keeping the British quiet and the taxes rolling in. If so, such pro-Roman leaders were soon to face the fury of their fellow Britons.

Hate was fanned into revolt in A.D. 60 by the Roman treatment of the Iceni. Prasutagus, the client king, died, having made the new Emperor, Nero, co-heir with his own two daughters. Roman officials on the spot, however, plundered the kingdom, seized Iceni land, made its leaders slaves and, in what was clearly an act of calculated insult, flogged Boudica, the late king's widow, and raped the two daughters. Boudica now raised an army said to number 120,000. As a client (not a conquered) tribe, the Iceni had retained their arms and, we must presume, their war chariots. Moving south they were joined by other disaffected natives, notably the Trinovantes. They made for the hated Colonia Victricensis, where the Temple of Claudius was a particular object of British loathing.

The main Roman army was currently campaigning on the Isle of Anglesey and a small

10   A large bronze head of the Emperor Claudius, apparently wrenched from an equestrian statue, found in the River Alde in Suffolk, could have been taken by Boudica's followers and ritually drowned in the aftermath of the destruction of the Roman colony.

force sent to the Colonia from London was of little help. The Britons destroyed the Colonia, killing everyone they found, systematically burning the place to the ground. Dramatic evidence of this has been demonstrated by archaeology. The 'Boudican destruction layer' is found everywhere. So fierce was the fire that clay walls and foundations have been baked solid. Charred textiles, burnt couches and incinerated floorboards have been uncovered, along with more general evidence of fire. Sometimes the layer is 30 cm. deep. Charred grain, flax, coriander, lentils and figs have been found. A bag of 23 dates (and one plum), the only ones known in Britain, had been completely carbonised. On what is still Colchester High Street a hardware shop was

11 Boudica rides on: as the logo of the *Essex County Standard*, Colchester's weekly newspaper.

full of imported stock. Glass vessels, doubtless from the Rhineland, stacked on the upper shelves, had melted and run down over nests of samian bowls, imported from Gaul, sealing them all together. Nearby a possible warehouse was stocked with 80 flagons and 30 grinding bowls. Yet in all this destruction virtually no bodies have been found. Some residents must have escaped; others were perhaps led away. Tacitus tells us that those Romans still present fled to the Temple of Claudius as a last refuge, but this too was finally torched and those inside were slaughtered.

Boudica's army now descended on the new port of Londinium (London) recently founded on the Thames to accommodate the vast flow of goods to and from the continent. We must assume that Camulodonum's River Colne was inadequate for the task. With London also destroyed, the Britons moved to Verulamium, the old tribal capital, now also a Roman town, and destroyed that too. There were atrocities. Roman power in Britain stood on the brink.

The governor, Suetonius Paulinus, rushed south, gathered an army and defeated the British in a great and bloody set-piece battle. According to Tacitus, Boudica committed suicide. Prolonged and severe reprisals followed. Roman writers hint at famine: standing crops may have been destroyed; new seeds had not been sown, the Britons having hoped to seize the Roman military granaries. The whole episode may have cost hundreds of thousands of lives. Roman advance in Britain was set back a decade.

Colonia Victricensis was, of course, rebuilt. The Gosbecks complex also survived. Indeed, as yet there is no archaeological evidence of destruction there. But no more prestige British burials are found at Stanway. Cooperation with the local British aristocracy was clearly a thing of the past.

The Boudican Revolt may have accelerated a process that was perhaps inevitable: the transfer of the capital of the new province from Colchester to London. Its far superior port facilities were central to its future; the road network radiating from it one of the long-term legacies of Roman rule. The site of Camulodunum had been chosen by Cunobelin and his predecessors as a compromise between a land route to their tribal heartland and a river route to the continent. Cunobelin thereby ensured that when the Emperor Claudius arrived, the new Colony of the Victorious, a city standing on a hill, would be built there too. Today, Colchester's High Street and Head Street follow lines set down by a legionary fortress 1,960 years ago, but it was not going to remain the capital of Britain.

Cunobelin, Claudius and Boudica: Colchester was never going to be so important again.

Two

The Roman Town
A.D. 60-450

❖

Roman Colchester lasted in some form for over 350 years. Enormous changes took place over this time, yet, after the dramatic events of Boudica's Revolt, Colchester scarcely appears in contemporary accounts of Britain, far less in the wider history of the Roman Empire. We are almost entirely dependent on archaeology and inferences drawn from events elsewhere. Archaeology has done wonderfully well, but the gaps are still enormous. Above all, few individuals rise to our view, no datable historic event is known.

The rebuilding of Colonia Victricensis must have been an exacting undertaking, not least because London and Verulamium had to be rebuilt too, though in the latter case this appears to have begun 15 years later. Who paid for the rebuilding? It was standard Roman practice to require the native population of any conquered province to finance its own development from taxation. The devastated Colonia still sat within the larger Camulodunum, though it may be that the former native capital now formed part of the 'territorium' of the Colonia.

Indeed, the defeated Trinovantes were treated so harshly that informed opinion doubted whether the area could provide the economic surplus needed to support the new province. Following an official enquiry prompted by the procurator responsible for financial affairs in Britain, the governor himself was recalled to Rome and replaced by someone more sympathetic to the need for future cooperation between Rome and the native population.

Meanwhile we must assume that the inhabitants of the rebuilt Colonia were all Roman citizens, mostly the retired legionary soldiers who traditionally settled there. Many indeed may have been survivors of the uprising. Archaeology suggests that some houses were rebuilt very quickly, often on the same building plots. There appears to have been no coordinated overall rebuilding. Indeed, the number of houses was now fewer, and gaps in the street lines more common. Normal services were resumed

12 How Colchester's Roman wall was built. Today, erosion of the outer courses of tiles and septaria stone means that along some stretches only the rubble core remains.

long, with battlements and towers at every street intersection, they were a major engineering undertaking. A core of mortar and septaria stone was faced on both sides by alternating courses of tiles and septaria which must have been dug out in great quantities from nearby coastal sites. And a conservative calculation suggests that almost 500,000 large, kiln-fired tiles (Roman bricks) were also used. The wall included six gates, the largest of which, the present Balkerne Gate, accommodated the main road to London. A large monumental double arch, perhaps commemorating the conquest by Claudius, was embraced by flanking towers, pedestrian exits and guard houses.

So vast an undertaking would have taken years to complete and was not solely defensive; it was psychological too. Colonia Victricensis had been built to persuade the British of the desirability of civilised, urban living. It had spectacularly failed, becoming instead the focus of an accumulated hatred; this must not happen again. The rebuilt Colonia was thus a statement. Town walls create a sense of awe; they carry prestige; they announce a secure, privileged inside, ring-fenced and Roman. This in turn may have contributed to Colchester's decline relative to London. A town of retired legionaries, seeking a quiet life, was not planning new economic initiatives. London's rise and rise was not due solely to its river facilities. London was full, said Tacitus, of merchants: thrusting, cosmopolitan, go-getting, perhaps already anticipating the rat race of the 21st-century City. Colchester's colonia, by contrast, reflected the retirement atmosphere of a modern Eastbourne.

Construction and psychology were also applied at Gosbecks, the tribal centre. Gryme's Dyke, today the western boundary of Colchester, was once assumed to be pre-Roman. Coins and pottery under its base now show that it was probably built by the Romans after the Boudican Revolt to defend the Gosbecks site

13 The southern bastion of the Balkerne Gate, uncovered to its foundation, demonstrating how the stone and tile courses of the Roman wall have been heavily eroded by time.

slowly. One undertaking, however, was quite exceptional: the building of a massive wall round the Colonia's perimeter.

The Roman historian Tacitus clearly states that Boudica's army had walked into Colchester 'because it had no walls'. This was not to happen again. Archaeologists now consider that Colchester's town walls, the first in Britain, date from the period A.D. 70-85. Originally over six metres high, 2.4 metres thick and 2,800 metres

14 The re-creation group, the Ermine Street Guard, pose at the Balkerne Gate, reflecting the part played by Colchester's Roman past in its modern image.

15 Artist Peter Froste's painting of the theatre built at Gosbecks.

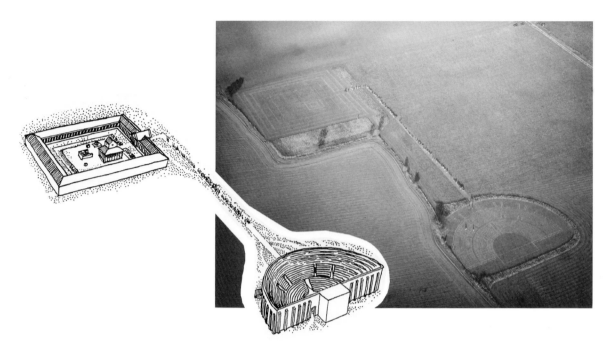

16 Aerial photograph using schoolchildren and the actual foundations of the Gosbecks temple and theatre marked on the grass, to illustrate, as in the drawing on the left, how the temple and theatre might be linked by ceremonial processions.

and the Roman town. A large theatre capable of accommodating 5,000, the largest theatre known from Roman Britain, was also built adjacent to the old royal farmhouse. Its unusual design suggests more an assembly place for public ceremony than a venue for theatrical performance. Two hundred metres from the theatre, the tribal 'sacred site' was surrounded by a massive square portico (covered walkway), its outer wall almost a quarter of a mile long, if measuring all four sides. Set inside the portico was a temple, made up of an outer walkway and an inner sanctum, of a type called 'Romano-Celtic', since it probably related to native traditions. Nor is it difficult to imagine how the temple, portico and theatre might be linked in civic, religious and other communal ceremonies, with processions from one to the other. An extensive water supply was also provided. All this suggests that British cultural life continued at Gosbecks, but was now given, to an extent

we cannot quantify, a Roman makeover. Great effort was being made to support British cultural distinction but in a way acceptable to, indeed orchestrated by, Rome.

The Romans had always sought to accommodate local religions by merging existing deities with their own. The discovery at Gosbecks (by a ploughman) of a magnificent bronze statuette of Mercury, the god of, among other things, commerce, suggests that the temple might be linked to this Roman god and Gosbecks might be a British trading area too. But, as Philip Crummy has argued, the statue, whose arms have been removed, might just as well be part of a later metalsmith's buried hoard from the days when Gosbecks had ceased to function; why else did so splendid a piece of artwork avoid appropriation in antiquity?

After A.D. 100 the Gosbecks theatre had its walls re-built in stone – its original wooden ones no doubt needed replacing – but around

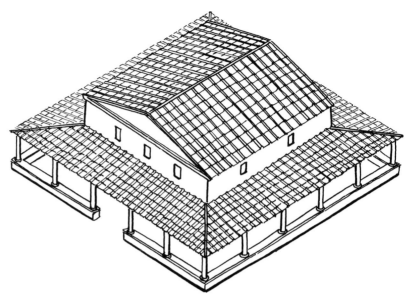

17 The bronze statuette of Mercury found by a ploughman on the outskirts of the Gosbecks site. The arms were removed in antiquity.

18 Drawing of a Romano-Celtic temple, datable to the second century, excavated in the Sheepen area.

19-20 Two tombstones of Roman soldiers, both broken across the base, possibly during Boudica's rising. Marcus Favonius Facilis, left, of the XXth Legion, was a centurion; Longinus Sdapeze, right, was a cavalry officer from the area of modern Bulgaria. His horse tramples down a cowering native Briton.

21 The so-called Colchester Vase, made in the town about A.D.150, shows two fighting gladiators: indeed their names have been scratched above their images on the rim of the vase. Memno, right, holds up a finger in submission to the fully armed Valentinus, left, who was attached to the XXXth Legion. The vase may commemorate an actual contest.

A.D. 200 it was demolished. We must assume that the Roman/British divide so sensitive after A.D. 60 was no longer meaningful. Gosbecks had ceased to be 'a tribal centre'. The residents of Camulodunum were now Romano-British.

We can also see a corresponding change after the Boudican revolt at the Sheepen site. Its manufacturing activity seems to have declined and in its place a number of Romano-British temples were built. Five have been identified so far, and there may have been more. This again suggests Roman accommodation with British traditions, marking a clear distinction between Roman civilisation within the walled town, native tradition without. Such a distinction, however, may not have lasted more than a generation. A considerable suburb soon developed outside the walls, spreading west along the road leading to London and another road leading towards the Sheepen area. To the west also lay an expanding cemetery, its finer monuments, in true Roman fashion, lining the route. Perhaps because they were broken and buried during the Boudican Revolt, two such tombstones survive today.

Although we can define with some certainty the street grid of the Roman town, the survival of modern Colchester on top of it has left many gaps in our knowledge. As a major Roman town the Colonia would have had a permanent water supply. Colchester stands on a hill; no Roman wells have been found within the walls. All this points to an aqueduct, water wheels or pressurised pumping system probably from the many springs to the west of the town. Conduits have been found in the area, underground water mains ran under the Balkerne Gate, lead pipes lay in modern Wyre Street and a building now in Castle Park, which filled with water when excavated, may have been a waterworks. Constant flowing water would be needed for public baths and we are still not sure where they were. The same water would have been used to take away sewage and sustain drainage.

Another puzzle is the site of the Colonia's forum and its accompanying basilica, the town's administrative centre. One suggestion is that it lay due south of the Temple of Claudius, forming part of an area of public buildings on the town's east. Alternatively, based on other Roman towns, the forum would have been on the intersection of the two main north-south, east-west roads, in which case it lies today under St Peter's Church and its churchyard.

Based on the details of its written charter, the Colonia would have been run by a council or *ordo* made up of up to 100 *decurions*, Roman citizens over 30, initially elected but, by the second century, selected, as it became harder to find volunteers to do the job. The *ordo* elected two sets of two magistrates to run affairs for a year. The senior ones dealt with minor criminal offences, the junior had responsibilities for public buildings, ceremonies and the Imperial cult. Taxes were a major concern: a land tax based on productivity and a poll tax on movable property and trade. There were also special levies for the army, always an important force in Britain which had the largest provincial army in the Empire.

A town peopled initially by ex-soldiers changed over time. It is possible that Colonia Victricensis became the preferred retirement home for members of the XXth Legion, which remained based in Britain for over a century. The Army recruited throughout the Empire and had always been a major source of new Roman citizens. Increasingly, however, the British upper class began to learn Latin, to have it taught to their children and to aspire to citizenship. Bilingualism must have become a characteristic of the town. This is important for, in the absence of a credible alternative, Colonia Victricensis must also have served as the tribal capital of the Trinovantes. This would have meant a duplicate council and duplicate sets of magistrates. Did they initially function at Gosbecks? Whatever the system – and we can assume there were many changes as time passed – it would have drawn more Britons into 'the Roman way of life'. By the time the Emperor Caracella, in 212, declared all freeborn residents of the Empire to be Roman citizens, old distinctions must have faded. We can envisage the Colonia now as a Romano-British community with a considerable ethnic mix: retired soldiers drawn from all quarters of the Empire, traders from many parts of Britain, particularly London, merchants from Gaul, provincial civil servants and country people with only a smattering of Latin bringing their produce to market.

Inside the Temple of Claudius there would have been a statue of Claudius, the Emperor God, probably more than life-sized. In front of the Temple, steps led down to a large courtyard at the far side of which stood a sacrificial altar, fronted by an elaborate screen, probably flanked by statues. There was of course a secular aspect to the Imperial cult, an expression of loyalty to the Roman state. But the complex cycle of ceremonies and festivals was promoted by a council elected or chosen by the native people. They annually nominated the chief priest, who would live in the cult centre for the year. Much of that ceremonial was paid for by him. The office was thus one likely to be taken up by the *nouveaux riches,* anxious to cover a humble background with a Roman veneer. Buildings to the south of the temple courtyard, perhaps associated with the town's basilica, would have served as the provincial headquarters of the cult. It is possible – we do not know – that this was later transferred to London.

Adjacent to the Temple stood a theatre, one of the few known in Roman Britain. Today it can be viewed in Maidenburgh Street. Its closeness to the Temple recalls that other temple and theatre combination at Gosbecks: one Imperial, one native, both likely to be associated with religious events. The Colonia theatre, however, could also have seen recitations, mimes, and classical plays with face masks, music and often vulgar story lines. Set into a hillside, the theatre was built so that an audience looked down onto the stage. Whether it also staged gladiatorial combat, wild animals and blood sports is doubtful. The Colonia's residents were certainly familiar with such 'sports': decorated bowls, figurines and painted domestic wall plaster found in Colchester all show gladiatorial scenes. However, no amphitheatre capable of housing them has yet been found.

Shopping would have provided another important part of town life; this was Britain's first consumer society. Though few have been specifically identified, workshops of all kinds would have doubled up as retail outlets. Food, clothes and domestic items, few of which survive in the archaeological record, would have been drawn from all over the Empire. A fragment of silk from China has been found in a local burial. Oysters from somewhere in Britain certainly reached Rome. The building and carpentry trades would have been kept busy. This included artists employed to paint murals on the walls of the dining room. There would have been workers in leather and metal. We know of one local coppersmith called Cintusmus, since he dedicated a plaque to the god Silvanus Calliros, a mix of native and classical names, at a temple near the present Grammar School.

Among the 15 tonnes of pottery fragments unearthed in excavations between 1971 and 1990 are examples from sites all over the Roman Empire, ranging from the famous Samian tableware manufactured in South Gaul (today France) to giant amphorae carrying wine from the Nile valley. Even so, two-thirds of that 15 tonnes was made locally, mostly to the west of the town outside the main built-up area, particularly from the mid-second to the mid-third centuries. Nearly 50 pottery

22 High status Samian-ware found in Colchester.

kilns have been discovered and there would have been far more. They include the only significant kiln in Britain to make the red slip Samian ware, a complex undertaking, the potters themselves being immigrants from the main manufacturing area in Gaul. In particular, Colchester potters specialised in *mortaria* or grinding bowls. Examples found at forts on

23 One of many mosaic floors uncovered in Colchester. This one was excavated in 1925 in the garden of 19, North Hill.

Hadrian's Wall probably reflect a lucrative army contract. The larger concerns must have been substantial family businesses. This would explain why five different persons with the name Sextus Valerius made Colchester *mortaria*.

The Colonia also provided the specialist services of lawyers and tutors, surveyors, translators and money lenders. Eventually the services of those who laid mosaic floors would also be called for, as large houses appeared. As the second century progressed a significant number of citizens prospered to the point where they could build larger, more luxurious houses with more rooms, stone-lined cellars, hypocaust heating, mosaic floors and even an upper storey. Such houses were invariably built round central courtyards in truly Roman style, suggesting that their owners were widely travelled, perhaps senior servants of the Empire or wealthy merchants who made the Colonia their home in retirement. Even the smaller houses were built of better material and, in consequence, lasted longer. Despite the restriction placed on archaeology by the presence of a modern town, over 50 mosaic floors have been identified in Colchester, a remarkable high number for a town of its size. For this is another characteristic of Colonia Victricensis in its third-century maturity: it had fewer houses and therefore fewer inhabitants than in its pre-Boudican heyday. A good deal of open space existed within the walls, much of it probably given over to cultivation. This doubtless explains the large granary built where today the Culver Precinct stands.

By this date, of course, Britannia was conquered. London was a great city. The northern frontier had been consolidated on Hadrian's Wall and the province had survived the experience of having its governor, Albinus, declare himself Emperor, taking the entire provincial army to Gaul to fight for his lost cause. We have no idea if the disruption this created in the north affected Colchester, as the new Emperor, Septimus Severus, arrived in York, the new northern capital, where he died in 211. Britannia was now divided into two provinces, the southern ruled from London, the northern from York, but this probably had little effect on Colchester.

The third century was marked throughout the Roman Empire by persistent inflation, as the army became more expensive to fund. The cost of the Imperial civil service was also a burden. Infrastructure and public works suffered. From the late third century a growing number of security problems plagued the west. In 260 a breakaway empire – the Gallic Empire – was formed of Britain, Gaul, Spain and Germany. Its collapse was followed in 277-9 by a revolt led by the governor of Britain, which was put down by German 'barbarians' recently settled in the province. Such barbarian communities were becoming widespread throughout the Empire, often in exchange for their military support, but time was to show that military support might not be the only consequence.

Civil War hit Britain again in 286 when Carausius, a discredited naval commander, seized

24 This decorated military buckle of the late Roman period found in Colchester might reflect the recruitment of barbarian soldiers.

control of Britain, and was in turn killed by his associate Allectus, who continued to rule his breakaway state until Constantius (father of the future Emperor Constantine) invaded Britain in 296 and reunited it with Rome. By now the majority of Roman towns in Britain were protected by walls, but in Colchester the threat of civil war saw the defences strengthened by blocking off two of the gates, including the Balkerne Gate, and digging a far deeper ditch round the town's perimeter. This also coincided with a growing threat of barbarian attack from the sea, particularly from the Saxons in north Germany. A long chain of defensive forts (Forts of the Saxon Shore) was built from Brancaster in Norfolk to Portchester in Hampshire. The relevant fort in Essex at Othona (today Bradwell-on-Sea) appears to date from around 270.

The reinforcing of Colchester's defences coincided with or accelerated the destruction of suburbs outside the walls. Few remained into the fourth century. Indeed, throughout the Colonia the removal of houses without any subsequent rebuilding is very marked after 300. Before 325 a massive aisled barn was built in the Culver Street area, evidence perhaps

25 Victorian enthusiasts systematically excavated many graves from the large Roman cemetery extending along Lexden Road. Many contained vessels and small figures presumably owned by the deceased. This collection, drawn by the artist Josiah Parish, came from one grave.

that this whole sector was now given over to cultivation and that self-sufficiency in grain had a high priority. It is difficult to avoid the conclusion that things were running down, indeed that the population of the town was falling. Among mosaics, for example, scarcely any date from after 300.

This said, we have clear evidence in the town's Roman cemeteries of fourth-century life. In 313 the Emperor Constantine confirmed the Edict of Milan, allowing freedom of worship for all Christians, of which, famously, he was one. The new Emperor's faith is generally reckoned

26 A wide variety of high quality Roman glassware has been found in Colchester. These came from the Butt Road cemetery.

to have been encouraged by his mother, Helena (later St Helena), a devout Christian, to whom a host of miraculous discoveries was later credited. We mention this now since we will meet St Helena again in a later chapter.

In Colchester careful excavation of the Butt Road cemetery has revealed 600 burials showing tell-tale Christian signs: a general lack of grave goods and the east-west lie of the bodies. Many of the interments also appear to be in family groups. A number of more affluent burials are in lead coffins, several where the body has been covered in plaster, perhaps to preserve it. Foundations can also be seen outside today's police station of what is almost certainly a Christian church associated with this cemetery, used for funeral services and memorial feasts, evidenced by the pig and chicken bones in its floor. The church appears to have remained in use well into the fifth century. At this date a pit was dug near the apse where two iron vessels and a knife, which presumably related to the funeral feasts, had been buried along with the skull and femur of an elderly woman who had survived a depressed fracture of the skull. Were these perhaps holy relics from the last days of Roman Colchester?

Some of the town's Romano-British temples also appear to have been demolished, possible evidence of Christian activity. Others, however, have not. Nor is there any real evidence for the suggestion that the Temple of Claudius became a Christian church. Basically, we just do not know what was happening as we move into the twilight world of late Roman Colchester.

The danger of settling barbarians in the Empire was vividly illustrated when Aleric and the Goths sacked Rome itself in 410. In Britain at the same date three successive usurpers seized power in quick succession. The last, Constantine III, crossed to Gaul, taking most of the Roman garrison with him. Britons in consequence had to make new terms with the barbarians, particularly the Saxons. Coin ceased to circulate; taxes were not collected; there was no army to pay. Roman law no longer operated; Britain had left the Roman Empire. Romano-British life nevertheless continued for some time. In 429, for example, two bishops from Gaul visited the shrine of St Alban at Verulamium and addressed the Christian community there. Probably until around 450 Romano-British rulers stayed in control of large areas of southern Britain.

Lying close to the Saxon shore, it is likely that the Colonia and its hinterland was settled early by Saxon immigrants, perhaps defended by Saxon mercenaries. The Romano-British community would seek to keep urban life going, and, as with other Roman towns in Britain, there is little evidence for a dramatic end to Roman Colchester. Signs of fire at the blocked 'Duncan's Gate' (now in Castle Park) could have several explanations and do not mean that the gates were 'stormed' by Saxons. Rather, Roman Colchester simply ground to a halt as the old way of life died. The number of residents would have dwindled as the former Colonia offered increasingly little apart from its defensive walls.

Two archaeological finds must serve to mark this transition. In 1964 a hoard of 15 silver

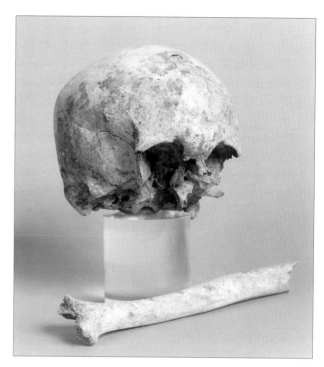

27 The skull and thigh bone of the elderly woman found placed within the Christian church now exposed outside Colchester police station. Note that she has survived a depressed fracture of the skull.

coins, buried by someone who never lived to collect them, was found near Artillery Folley, 300 metres south of the walled town. They date to 407-11 and have been heavily 'clipped' – slivers of silver have been cut from their rims. Since clipping was a serious crime, the coins must date to after the breakdown of Roman rule. The second find is the foundations of a Saxon hut, datable to the mid-fifth century, found during the extensive archaeological dig at Lion Walk in 1972.

The coins and the hut show that, though Roman urban life had ceased, handfuls of people continued to live in the half-ruined town. The same appears to be true of the next few hundred years, the so-called Dark Ages, after the Saxons took over.

Three
From Saxons to Normans
450-1200

We know very little about Colchester between the years 400 and 900. This is an immense period of time, though not one dominated by towns. Colchester, however, did not cease to exist; indeed, developments took place which were to affect the rest of its history. The steady influx of Saxon and Fresian migrants to Britain appears to have reached a critical point around 450. An era of conflict led to most of southern and eastern Britain passing under their tribal control. Saxons lived an agrarian life, were pagan and illiterate, clustered in small communities of thatch-covered wooden huts. Over time, family groups were amalgamated into larger units till all the land between the Stour and the Thames formed the kingdom of the East Saxons, giving the county of Essex its name and its boundaries.

We know next to nothing about their history, but the East Saxons made English the dominant local language and supplied most of our place-names. In the case of Colchester the name seems to be based on 'Colonia-cester', meaning 'Colonia camp', an interesting echo of the Roman past, rather than 'Colne-cester', the 'camp on the River Colne'. Saxon burials, often on the fringe of the Roman cemeteries, fragments of pottery, bone combs, beads, bronze brooches, loom weights, spear heads, a sword or two, at least three huts, even two coins, all dating from the fifth to the eighth centuries, show that Saxons were living in Colchester throughout this period, though probably in small numbers and in a distinctly rural setting. How far the town formed a local market or the base for a tribal leader we do not know, but both must be possible. The old Temple of Claudius, for example, could have provided the stronghold for a warlord.

In 653, as the Anglo-Saxon kingdoms began to embrace Christianity, St Cedd was sent as missionary to the East Saxons. As bishop he built his main church at Bradwell-on-Sea beside the Saxon Shore fort of Othona. His successors, however, were based in London, now the chief

28 Dark-Age evidence for life going on in Colchester: a fifth-century brooch, a discarded sixth- or seventh-century comb and a coin datable to *c*.720.

town of the East Saxon kingdom and, until 1846, Essex remained part of the diocese of London. Once more London robbed Colchester of a major role. The East Saxon kingdom was never very powerful, usually recognising the kings of Mercia in the Midlands as their overlords. Nevertheless London, the former Roman city and centre of a surviving road network, would have given the East Saxons strategic significance.

Saxon London is therefore important in understanding Colchester. Between the seventh and ninth centuries a string of new trading sites or 'wics' grew up, doing business with what is now France and the Low Countries. Lundenwic (London) sat outside the Roman city, most of which lay uninhabited. Yorvic was the former York, Hamwic the future Southampton, while a new port grew up just north of Colchester at Gipeswic, today Ipswich, which, during the forthcoming period of Danish rule, prospered in its role as a southern outpost of a North Sea economy.

Colchester was thus denied a significant role in the economic, administrative and religious framework established in the mid-Saxon

29 Peter Froste's reconstruction of a seventh-century Saxon hut, apparently used for weaving, built against a Roman foundation wall and found during the excavations at Lion Walk.

period. It would never be a cathedral city or a county town, and the rise of Ipswich further demonstrated its shortcomings as a port. Other former Roman towns, such as Canterbury, Winchester and York, provided power bases for royal households and for the emerging Church hierarchy, conscious of its

30 A replica Viking ship used at a re-creation of the 991 Battle of Maldon.

31 The tower of Holy Trinity Church, datable to *c*.1000, may have initially served as an observation tower.

historic Roman legacy. Colchester could only fall back on its potential as a stronghold behind its Roman walls.

That potential became real as the Anglo-Saxon kingdoms came under assault from Danes and Vikings, as the Scandinavian raiders were called. From 850 the raiders became invaders, culminating in the arrival of the Danish Great Army in 865. Within three years the kingdoms of East Anglia and Northumbria had been conquered and the Stour, the northern boundary of Essex, had become a frontier. By now the East Saxon kingdom had been absorbed by the West Saxons, the last East Saxon king being expelled in 825. As a new Danish army advanced against Wessex, King Alfred finally drove them back, negotiating a truce with the Danish leader Guthrum in

878, which left Eastern England under Danish rule.

Danish settlements seem to have remained north of the Stour. A handful of Danish place-names hugs the mouth of its estuary. The Essex town of Harwich perhaps commemorates the 'wic' where a Danish 'here' or fighting force was based. Colchester had earlier been a defended Wessex settlement, but after 878 it clearly came under Danish military occupation, though its Saxon population may have remained. In 913 Alfred's successor, Edward the Elder, came with an army into Essex and camped at Maldon, establishing a large fort at Witham. In 917, assisted by the men of Essex, Edward stormed and took Colchester, killing the Danish garrison, 'except', the Anglo-Saxon Chronicle notes, 'the men who fled ... over the wall'. Edward returned to Colchester later that year with the West Saxon army and 'repaired and restored the borough where it had been broken'.

This may have involved more than mending the walls. Wessex strategy in driving back the Danes was based on securing well-defended, planned towns. Colchester was ideally suited for this and its modern street pattern, north and south of High Street, suggests some deliberate re-planning. The break with the past is clear in that none of the old Roman streets were re-used except High Street and Head Street-North Hill, the main axes of the town, and Queen Street, all leading to gateways. Indeed, the earlier blocking off of the Balkerne Gate meant that, as today, High Street stopped where it met Head Street.

Colchester now became a strategic centre once more. In 926 Athelstan, son and successor to Edward the Elder, captured York from the Vikings and united all England under one king. In 931 Athelstan held a meeting of the royal council or 'witan' at Colchester, attended by at least 13 earls (of whom six were Danes), three abbots, 15 bishops and the Archbishop of Canterbury. Where did they meet? One

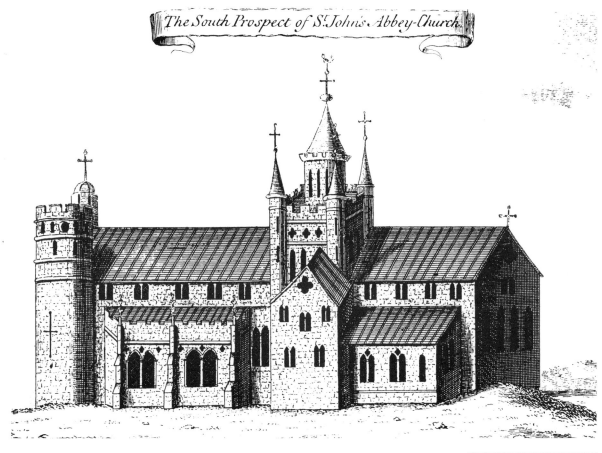

The South Prospect of St Johns Abbey-Church

establishment in Essex, a considerable power in its own right, and a source of employment. Scheregate Steps, a medieval breach through four metres of Roman wall, may have begun as a short cut for townsmen working at the abbey. Finally, early in the new century, on a green-field site on the road to the Hythe port, Eudo founded St Mary Magdalen Hospital (see page 29), initially for lepers, but later for the sick in general.

Almost simultaneously, in about 1100, the group of priests serving St Botolph's Church transformed it into the first (and therefore senior) Augustinian Priory in Britain. Never wealthy on the scale of St John's Abbey, St Botolph's was always a small foundation, but, as it rose slowly to completion over the next 77 years, it produced a Norman church of

33 The church of St John's Abbey from a drawing of 1463, showing a core Norman building with later Gothic additions.

34 Though no likeness of Eudo the Dapifer survives, his statue on Colchester Town Hall supplies a contemporary identity.

35 The earliest known Colchester borough seal, dating from around 1200, emphasises the castle and the fishery: see the fish below the castle.

some style and some size, the ruins of which still survive. It too was built in large part from recycled Roman building material.

An abbey, a monastery, a hospital and a royal castle added to Colchester's status as an important town. At this stage that status was based less on successful trade and more on institutional prestige and strategic importance. Eudo Dapifer is without doubt one of the

36 St Helena's Chapel, standing on the foundations of the Roman Theatre, was extensively restored in the Victorian period.

major figures in Colchester's history. He left the town more prosperous and probably more contented than he had found it, an accolade which not all Norman rulers earned. He was buried in St John's Abbey and his body was moved in 1320 from the chapter house to the newly built presbytery. His monument there might one day provide the highlight of an archaeological exploration.

As a borough of some substance and the home of a royal castle, Norman Colchester made early progress towards a degree of self government. Though it has not survived, it is clear that a charter was issued by Henry I recognising the town's rights and giving the burgesses power to appoint two bailiffs to conduct their affairs and balance their books. The charter probably included some recognition of the town's rights over the tidal River Colne and its fishery. Around 1160 a substantial stone moot hall was built with lavishly decorated windows and door on the site where earlier a lord's hall may have stood. Although demolished in 1843 (when it was the oldest moot hall in England) to accommodate a new, larger town hall, surviving drawings confirm its fine appearance.

In 1189 Richard I (the Lionheart) issued a further charter, the wording of which has survived. It confirms the town's right to elect two bailiffs, to hold its own courts of law, to control the river and the fishery and to be exempt from royal Forest Law. Colchester's market was protected from outside unlicensed markets, their citizens were free from courts outside the borough, and their merchants free from customary taxations elsewhere. These were significant rights.

We have already noted the prestige which Colchester carried as a former Roman town. Despite much use of Roman remains for building material, the evidences of the past were still visible. The old walls stood; Roman coin and pottery were constantly encountered in the ground. It is, therefore, not surprising

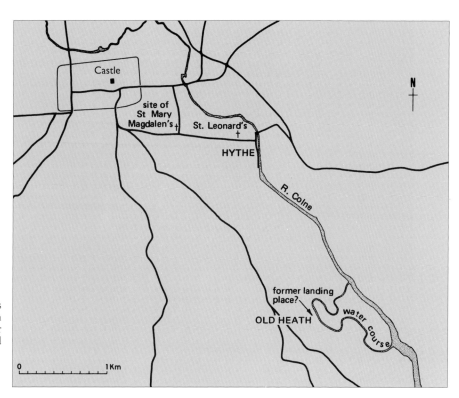

37 Map showing the sites of the Mary Magdalen Hospital and the former hythe (harbour) at Old Heath.

that this antique past was peopled by popular legend. One key figure was the fabled King (or Duke) Coel, who is surely not a real Dark-Age king, but an imaginary ruler derived from the town's name, invented to explain the impressive ruins. Thus, before its demolition, the Temple of Claudius was called King Coel's Palace and the Balkerne Gate was King Coel's Castle. In much the same way the old Camulodunum earthwork was called Gryme's (the Devil's) Dyke.

Popular legend, however, was transcended as King Coel became associated with the real figure of St Helena. We have already noted her devout Christianity and influence on her son, the Emperor Constantine. He, for his adoption of Christianity, was now regarded as one of the greatest individuals in history; she had already been credited with miraculously finding Christ's cross and the graves of the three Magi. Constantine had indeed had links with Britain, having been proclaimed Emperor at York, but St Helena has no known links.

Nevertheless, probably before 1066, Colchester developed the legend that Helena was the daughter of King Coel of Colchester, who, to prevent a war, married her to Constantine's father, the Roman Caesar Constantius. Colchester thus housed two chapels dedicated to St Helena, one of which, either the one still in Maidenburgh Street or the building in front of Colchester Castle, was 'restored' by Eudo Dapifer. It must, therefore, have been a Saxon foundation. St Helena has been with us ever since.

Though Colchester's pre-eminence rested more on locus than on trade, Norman drive provided one more vital feature of the town: a new port. The early Saxon Hythe – little more than a landing place – lay south of Colchester and is probably still recalled in the suburb of Old Heath (i.e. old hythe). The New Hythe (as it was called) was built one mile east of the town in a straight line from the Mary Magdalen Hospital. The wharves

38   Watercolour by Mary Benham inside a Norman stone house and undercroft which stood behind Colchester High Street until 1886.

and community of houses must have been established before 1150. It early acquired its own church, St Leonard's, which is mentioned in 1150, and its site some way up Hythe Hill suggests that houses already stretched that far from the river.

Simultaneous with the building of the Hythe there must have been a considerable effort to improve the river and eliminate some of the shoals and meanders, evidence of which survives in later maps. Though probably never able to take large ships of the period except at spring tides, Colchester's ability to provide credible port facilities was crucial to its future development. Colchester's merchant community had always to maintain a foothold at the Hythe

as well as in High Street over a mile away. Though none have survived today, we know of several substantial High Street stone houses of Norman date, some with stone cellars, built with recycled Roman tile and stone.

Commercialisation thus came to frame the future of the town quite as much as royal favour, but in this Colchester was less successful than others in the early Norman period. By the reign of Henry I it perhaps ranked only 27th among the provincial towns of England. Its size and facilities, however, were considerably greater than they had been before the Normans arrived and would provide a sound base on which a later medieval prosperity might be built.

Four

The Medieval Town
1200-1525

Throughout the Middle Ages Colchester was a town of national importance. As a stronghold of the great East Anglian cloth industry it also became a manufacturing centre of note. This, however, developed slowly. Though it continued to grow both physically and in terms of population, before the dramatic arrival of the Black Death in 1348 Colchester was far less dynamic than many of its smaller Essex neighbours and far less important as a trading centre than Ipswich. Nor, set so far in the north of Essex, could Colchester sustain the role of county town, given the quality of medieval roads. In consequence the new town of Chelmsford, established by the Bishop of London in 1200-5, developed rapidly into the normal centre for county business and the court of the itinerant royal justices. Chelmsford was helped by its proximity to the royal manor of Writtle, the seat of a royal palace.

Until 1250 Colchester Castle remained of major military significance in the defence of eastern England. Henry I, Henry II and Henry III all spent time here and King John was

39 This artistic impression of Colchester Castle in 1200 by Peter Froste gives it three floors. There may have been only two. Note, at the base of the castle, the small Saxon chapel, the foundations of which can be seen today. This strongly suggests there were other Saxon features destroyed when the castle was built.

40 These carvings on the walls inside the castle of a soldier, an archer and a fleur-de-lys, a key symbol in the French royal arms, might have been cut during the siege of 1215-16.

41 Aaron of Colchester, a caricature drawn in the margin of the Forest Roll when his sons were charged with other Colchester citizens for hunting a deer into the town. Note his Jewish 'badge'.

present on seven different occasions, ultimately at moments of national crisis. In November 1214 civil war threatened after John returned from France having failed to re-conquer his lands there. The Constable of the Castle, William de Lanvalai, who held the manor of Lexden, was a member of the baronial group opposed to the King. John came to Colchester, probably seeking to win over Lanvalai and other wavering barons. Leaving the castle in the hands of the Sheriff, Lanvalai joined the rebellious barons at Bury St Edmunds where they resolved to place their grievances before the King. Fearing its loss, the King sent one of his Flemish mercenaries, Stephen Harengood, to take over Colchester Castle and put the fortress in a state of defence.

Lanvalai joined the barons who now rode to London, forcing the King to accept Magna Carta at Runnymede in June 1215. As part of the agreement, which John regarded as a mere truce, Harengood had to surrender Colchester Castle. The King, however, continued to fight

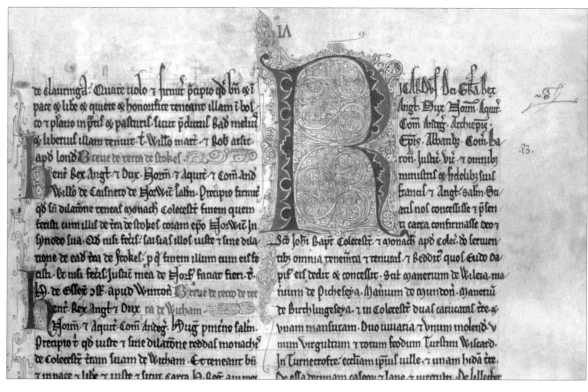

42 Anxious to keep records of their legal rights, St John's Abbey compiled an illuminated list of its charters, even concocting charters to cover rights not written down elsewhere. The large capital R begins those rights granted by King Richard I; the two small Hs show those of Henry I and Henry II.

his barons and later that year a detachment of French troops arrived to garrison the castle for the barons' cause. Having just subdued Rochester Castle, John promptly sent Savory de Meuleon to besiege Colchester Castle, even as baronial reinforcements arrived at Colchester. It was now mid-winter. In March the King himself appeared and secured a prompt surrender. The French negotiated a safe passage to London for 115 of their men – where they were promptly arrested. Thus ended the only military action that Colchester Castle ever saw. Though it had changed hands five times in just over a year, it had never been taken. A footnote came a few months later when a ragged baronial army arrived in Colchester and ravaged the town.

In 1217 as part of a new truce the French under Prince Louis, the heir to the French throne, briefly reoccupied the castle, before it reverted once more into royal hands. By 1350 the castle had ceased to have military significance, its chief role being that of a gaol. Until then it formed a world apart from Colchester, occasionally hosting the great and the fearsome, occasionally generating contracts for food, wine or timber on a royal scale.

Mention should also be made of Colchester's Jewish community, resident here from around 1150 until all Jews were expelled from the kingdom in 1290. By that date only some eight rather modest Jewish households remained in Colchester, though earlier men like Isaac of Colchester (died by 1209), who lent extensively to the Crown, were wealthy and well connected. There was a synagogue, a Jewish bailiff in charge of the Jewish community, a possible court house and such integration that a group of local Jews and Christians might end up together in court for taking a deer, illegally chased into the town itself.

Given the often violent nature of life in the early Middle Ages, Colchester was relatively free from attacks such as it suffered at the hands of the barons in 1216. It was, however, often enmeshed in conflict with its neighbours. Disagreements regularly arose between the town and St John's Abbey, who were lords of the manors of Greenstead and West Donyland. Constant bickering occurred over grazing, the abbot's right to erect a gallows and his rights in the warren at West Donyland where rabbits, a Norman introduction, were harvested as a source of meat. The abbey also held estates scattered around the Liberties (Colchester's outer parishes), providing further cause for friction and rival authorities. Rights of common were particularly contested, being of vital importance to the poor of Colchester as population grew and enclosures reduced available pasture.

For agriculture probably still represented the main economic interest of the town, just as the round of winter, seedtime and harvest governed its civic calendar and annual fairs. Despite sporadic efforts by the bailiffs to control them, pigs ran in the streets. A high proportion of Colchester burgesses was engaged in both farming and commerce, and the Liberties, the rural parishes of Mile End, Lexden, West Donyland and Greenstead, would have provided much of the town's food supply. Much, but not all. Perhaps a quarter of the land round Colchester was given over to heath and woodland, from the extensive Tiptree Heath to the south through Lexden Heath to a swathe of heathland from Parson's Heath up to Dedham. Such land was too infertile for arable farming, providing instead rough pasture and scrub which was used for fuel, another issue of vital importance to the poor if it were restricted. Perhaps one-third of Mile End and Greenstead was covered in woodland, from the great King's Wood (today High Woods) through

Welshwood to Crockleford Wood. Deer were still common and a target for poachers; robbers lay in wait for travellers on the road to Ardleigh. Such woodland should not be viewed as 'waste' awaiting development. The limits of possible agriculture had already been reached; even heavy marshland along the Colne Estuary was subject to sophisticated crop rotations. In fact, woods were a vital source of grazing, fuel and timber, a resource which was 'farmed' as surely as a field of oats.

The mainly sandy soils round Colchester could not sustain an annual crop of wheat, the main bread grain, most of which was grown on land to the west. Through Colchester and across the Tendring Hundred rye was the common winter-sown crop, three times more common than wheat. Then there were the needs of pastoral farming. Sheep grazing on the marshes provided wool. Milk, cheese and dairy products came from the heathlands. Butchers and leather merchants looked to cattle fattened on meadows along river valleys and what passed in Essex for steep-sided pasture.

For all these reasons, before 1350 parishes up to an eight-mile radius helped to supply Colchester's food needs. But Colchester's population of 3,000-plus represented barely one-tenth of those resident in an area which included markets such as Manningtree, West Mersea, Brightlingsea, Coggeshall, Earls Colne and Dedham, which all had seafaring or manufacturing sectors of their own. Indeed, produce even left some coastal villagers for the supply of London. Colchester, therefore, did not dominate supplies in its own district, nor capture all marketable surpluses; and this in an age when dearth and the unrest it caused were recurring features of urban life.

One vital part of Colchester's economy was the sea and the tidal estuary of the Colne, with its narrow creeks and marshes. New Hythe sustained a small merchant fleet which offered employment to perhaps 200 men. But more important was fishing which provided a significant food source for Colchester market and the oysters which were abundant in the creeks and waters of the Colne. Up and down its length elaborate fish weirs and traps harvested the sea. This also generated controversy. In 1253 up to forty Colchester men, including leading burgesses, were accused of cutting the ropes of the abbot's ships and dismantling his gallows at West Donyland and Greenstead.

The abbey had the right to hold a trade fair on St John's Green outside the Abbey Gate at midsummer. At the 1272 fair trouble broke out between the abbot's men and the townsmen. Cutting a corpse down from their gallows, the abbot's men laid it on St John's Green, accusing the townsmen of murder. Only the borough's right to its own Coroner's Court enabled them to confound this story, the corpse being already 'stinking'. Was there an echo here of the confrontation of 19 years before? Certainly it suggests a popular hostility against the abbey as a rival centre of power.

Colchester might equally be 'at war' with its powerful baronial neighbours. A long-running dispute raged between the town and the formidable FitzWalter family, lords of the manor of Lexden and owners of land in London, Norfolk, Suffolk and Essex. The parish of Lexden had only become part of the Liberties of Colchester in the late Saxon period, and this had been challenged in the early Norman years. The FitzWalters therefore systematically dragged their feet, even as the borough sought to enforce its rights. In 1312 a number of townsmen, including several important ones, indulged in a deliberate trespass. Seizing his goods (or so Robert FitzWalter claimed), they entered Lexden Park and hunted there.

In 1343 there was a more serious dispute with his son, John, Lord FitzWalter. This time 96 named leading townsmen were accused of a similar invasion: cutting down trees, hunting deer, fishing in the lord's fishponds. A fracas

43 Norman and Saxon fish weirs existed on a grand scale. Foundations survive of an elaborate tidal weir like this, built by Saxons off Mersea Island. Drawing by Mark Nethercoat.

ensued during which, FitzWalter claimed, one of his servants was injured and died. Going to law, which of course the trespass was aimed to induce, FitzWalter tried to get one of Colchester's two bailiffs convicted of the offence. A juror who found him not guilty was severely beaten up and a second threatened juror just managed to flee. FitzWalter now terrorised Colchester from May to July, lying in wait for Colchester men going to market, until bought off with a lump sum of £40. He did the same the following spring, collecting a further £40. His steward helped himself to goods at Colchester market and FitzWalter refused to pay Lexden's part of Colchester's contribution to national taxation, saying he would break the arms and legs of any peasant who opposed him. In these circumstances Colchester needed all the allies it could get. A written agreement drawn up that same year with the abbot of St John's over the burgesses' claims to rights of common conceded all the points the abbey claimed.

Though Colchester's royal charters clearly laid claim to the entire fishery of the Colne from the Hythe to the sea, it was quite another matter to enforce these rights. Aggressive

44 One page of the long list of wills [Testamentum] enrolled in Colchester in 1348-9 during the Black Death.

riverside landlords were inclined to help themselves. Matters came to a head in 1350 when Lionel de Bradenham, a tenant of the FitzWalters and lord of the manor of Langenhoe, accused of placing 'six great weirs in the deep channel of the Colne', marched on Colchester with 200 men-at-arms and attacked the eastern suburbs. Windows and doors were smashed and residents, driven from their houses, fled into the town. Grain and hay were looted. Bradenham intended to set fire to the town but, meeting stiff resistance, settled down to besiege it until the following November. His followers were told to hunt down and kill any Colchester men they could find, sparing only those with passes issued by Bradenham. He summoned to

his aid a string of leading local landholders, several of whom were subsequently shown to have been building weirs themselves. Finally the town surrendered, buying Bradenham off for £20. Bradenham was no common criminal. A successful and innovative farmer, a lawyer and legal adviser, he had undertaken missions for the crown and was for a while acting constable of Colchester Castle. Clearly he had observed and learnt from the policy of the FitzWalters.

This then was Colchester in the mid-14th century. Neither economically strong nor rich, it was struggling to uphold its rights against brute force. Its 1313 population of 3-4,000 was probably now falling. It had slipped down the national league table to perhaps 46th among provincial towns. A 1334 taxation based on wealth saw it half the size of Ipswich and rated lower in Essex than Writtle, Barking and Waltham Holy Cross. Then came the catastrophe of the Black Death.

It is probably impossible today to comprehend the impact on a religious, indeed superstitious, world of a disease which killed between a third and a half of the population of Europe. In Colchester the impact can be seen in the 111 wills proved between September 1348 and September 1349 and the 25 in the year following, compared with an annual average of two to three. Clearly a lot of influential people feared they were going to die – and did, including, apparently, both the abbot of St John's and the prior of St Botolph's. We cannot quantify total deaths, partly because immigrants quickly took their place and often died too, but a 40 per cent mortality seems not unreasonable on the evidence.

The Cloth Trade

Against this discouraging background, Colchester's cloth industry began to expand. It had first emerged in the period after 1225 and early specialised in russet, a medium quality

THE WOOL TRADES

Shearing
Sheep were raised in large numbers on the coastal marshes of Essex, but wool from all over England was used for Colchester russets.

Dyeing
Dyeing was often done before the wool was spun. Woad and madder were the main dyes for russets. Colour variation came from dye strength and mix. Vegetable dyes required a mordant to fix the colour.

Combing and carding
After washing (warm water and urine), oiling and teasing, carding was the normal method of bringing short staple woollen fibres into line and then rolled to form a rolag for spinning. The wooden cards were curved and faced with thin metal 'teeth', the work of a specialist cardmaker. Combing was applied to long staple wool, pulling the wool through the teeth of a fixed comb. Combing was vital for preparing the long-staple fibres used in bays and says. Woolcombers or yarn makers were often small masters supervising their own spinners.

Spinning
The 'big wheel' was used for spinning from the late 13th century. It would turn on its own momentum (with help from a stick or hand), leaving both hands free for a while to 'draw out' the yarn. Portable wheels were common and women might be seen in groups, chatting and 'spinning a yarn'.

Weaving
Russets were woven on broad looms with hand-thrown shuttles. Colchester broadcloth was normally 2 yards wide, 12½ yards long.

cloth, usually grey, sometimes brown, dyed with woad and madder. Colchester mainly produced 'broad' cloth, 12 yards long and two yards wide. From 1249 Henry III regularly bought 'Colchester russets' for his household and as a named cloth it was soon being sought overseas. For 100 years, however, it remained a small concern. In the sluggish years of the early 14th century Colchester's leather-processing industry was of more importance.

Several factors enabled the cloth trade to grow after 1350. The disruptive effect of the Black Death offered new opportunities, as transport and labour costs rose. Colchester was

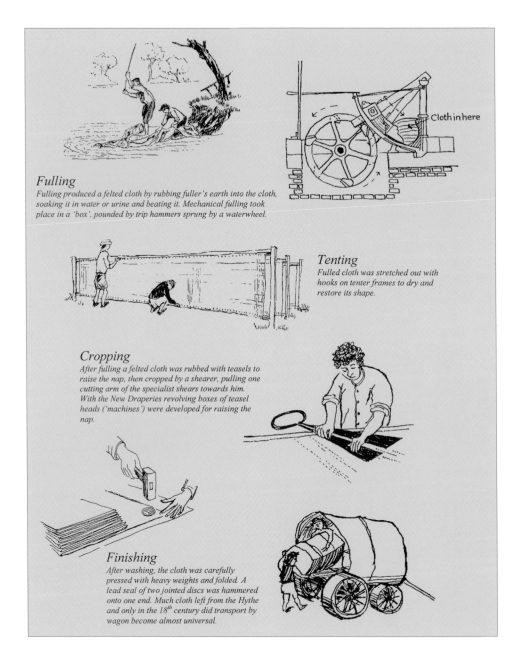

Fulling
Fulling produced a felted cloth by rubbing fuller's earth into the cloth, soaking it in water or urine and beating it. Mechanical fulling took place in a 'box', pounded by trip hammers sprung by a waterwheel.

Cloth in here

Tenting
Fulled cloth was stretched out with hooks on tenter frames to dry and restore its shape.

Cropping
After fulling a felted cloth was rubbed with teasels to raise the nap, then cropped by a shearer, pulling one cutting arm of the specialist shears towards him. With the New Draperies revolving boxes of teasel heads ('machines') were developed for raising the nap.

Finishing
After washing, the cloth was carefully pressed with heavy weights and folded. A lead seal of two jointed discs was hammered onto one end. Much cloth left from the Hythe and only in the 18th century did transport by wagon become almost universal.

able to produce competitively priced export-led cloth, first by its coastal location, second by developing mechanical fulling at a string of mills on the river, and thirdly from the lack of guilds among its weavers and fullers, enabling market forces to operate among the small capitalists taking up the industry.

They in turn had to find new markets and regular supplies of wool and develop a credit nexus among themselves. It is probably worth exploring these issues in turn.

Over the period 1350-1450 Colchester found its wool both locally and across southern England. Before long its midsummer wool fair even attracted London merchants. Wool was washed, scrubbed, broken up and combed or carded locally. Woad and other dyestuffs came into the Hythe, sometimes from overseas. So did fuller's earth. Wool was dyed 'in the wool' before being spun, usually on spinning wheels by women resident in the Liberties. Weaving on the broad loom with a hand-held shuttle was a male activity, undertaken in several ways. Weavers might work on contract, by the day or for piece rates. Most worked for several employers. Some, however, might buy wool, subcontract washing and dyeing, and work on their own account as small capitalists. Likewise some fullers put out wool to be dyed and yarn to be woven.

Fulling was done mechanically on the river in mills converted from grain milling, along the stretch downstream from North Bridge: North Mill, Middle Mill, Stokes Mill, New Mill, in that order. Later, there was a fulling mill at the Hythe too. The river banks and mill races could be seen, day and night, hanging with new cloths put out to dry. Depending on the finished product, cloth was soaked in animal urine and pounded in a 'box' by hammers triggered by water wheels. Before fulling one could see through the woven cloth; afterwards it was dense and matted. Fulled cloth was increasingly stretched to dry on tenter frames. Fullers might work on contract, for themselves, or even rent the use of a mill from an owner.

The finishing processes involved further skills. Shearers trimmed the nap of the cloth after it had been raised with teasels. Local taxes had to be paid and the cloth sealed with lead seals as part of a quality and marketing process. As time went by, less Colchester cloth was dyed but was sent to London plain. Colour dyeing could be a costly, specialist activity and russets were never the only local cloth. Most cloth appears to have been exported by Colchester men in English ships, considerably increasing activity at the Hythe: new quays were laid out and two treadmill cranes installed.

Three specialist overseas outlets were exploited by local merchants; little went through the established routes of the Low Countries. Since the early 14th century wine had been imported to Colchester from Gascony. Increasingly, russets went back by return, Gascony becoming the main outlet for Colchester cloth before 1400. Secondly, Colchester merchants pioneered a market in the Baltic, particularly with Prussia. In exchange came fish, wheat and timber, but also bitumen and wax, Swedish iron and German beer. Thirdly, Colchester cloth entered the Mediterranean, not directly in English ships, but via London, purchased as 'Essex cloth' by the London agents of the large Italian companies. In this way Colchester russets reached Tuscany and Spain and even Malaga, Damascus and the Black Sea.

Colchester by now sat on the fringe of a great cloth-making area stretching across north Essex and much of Suffolk. Inevitably this generated trading opportunities and access to pools of skill and capital. Despite the rival attraction of Ipswich and – to a growing extent – London, Colchester served as a port for some of this trade. It is also doubtless significant that in 1377 Colchester's casual wool fair, now held in both June and July, was restructured by William Rayne, one of the town's more dynamic figures, on far more formal lines: operated from the Moot Hall cellars, it was held in rented booths erected from the top of High Street to St Runwald's Church. By the late 1390s this was the largest cloth market in the Eastern Counties, larger even than Norwich. And it was still the largest in the 1460s.

Faced with sluggishness in its main markets, Colchester later produced a wider range of cloth of a higher quality, including blues and 'musterdevillers', a new type of grey. Undoubtedly the biggest change was the opening of new markets through Hamburg in the mid-15th century, operated from Colchester by the merchants of the great

45 John Ball, seen preaching on horseback, the 'rebel priest' of the Peasants' Revolt, had close Colchester connections.

Hanseatic League. For a while Hanse exports from Colchester exceeded those of London. This same process saw the Colchester industry more tightly regulated and concentrated in the hands of fewer, more wealthy merchants, such as Thomas Christmas I and Thomas Christmas II, father and son, the latter a key benefactor of Colchester's future Grammar School by his 1520 will. By 1500 Colchester's rich clothiers had in turn come under the control of London's far larger marketing agencies.

Cloth was thus Colchester's engine of change; everything else grew in its train. Population rose sharply. By about 1410 it had perhaps reached 8,000, placing Colchester firmly in the top ten towns in the kingdom. Colchester acquired more butchers, brewers and bakers, as well as more outsiders coming to sell goods in the town's marketplace. More visitors meant more inns to house them, more taverns to entertain them, more luxury imports at the Hythe.

Colchester's medieval golden age coincided with a rural crisis. Bubonic plague did not strike once; it struck often – in 1361, 1369, 1375, 1380, 1390 and on into the 15th century. At each outbreak rural immigrants filled the gaps left in the towns, and increasingly this left England, whose population may have almost halved, with fewer mouths to feed, fewer rural inhabitants and fewer labourers, forcing wages up. Consequently Colchester's population, once one-tenth of that within an eight-mile radius, was now one quarter. Longer distance food supplies were needed. Wheat (for milling) and barley (for brewing) came in at the Hythe, some of it from Europe. As more land became pastoral, cheaper wool could be sought nation-wide. Despite a drop in population to about 5,300, Colchester was still in 1525 about the tenth largest town in the kingdom.

One dramatic consequence of population crisis was the Peasants Revolt of 1381, which actually began in Essex. Colchester's relative affluence explains why the revolt found little support among its leaders. Protesters from the district attacked both the Moot Hall and St John's Abbey, seeking to destroy manorial records. Colchester's records survived, but no borough court met for five weeks. Probably the authorities lost control of the streets. Several Flemings were murdered, evidence of their unpopularity in the control of trade. Colchester's other contribution was to house the spin-doctor of rebellion, the priest John Ball, who in the years before the revolt was active in the district preaching his heretic doctrine of social equality. Wat Tyler, the peasants' leader, may also have had a Colchester connection. In the aftermath of the revolt some long overdue repairs were begun to the town walls, supplying the round bastions which can still be seen in Priory Street and Vineyard Street. Not that they were ever tested. Colchester was never caught in the middle of a conflict between the Crown and the private army of an 'over-mighty subject'. Like most medieval towns, it steered clear of national politics and the factional disputes of the Wars of the Roses.

The tenth largest town in Britain also housed great poverty. Perhaps one-third of its

46 Bastions in modern Priory Street, added to strengthen the rebuilt town walls in the 1380s.

inhabitants formed the absolute poor, transient, desperate and vulnerable to disease. But medieval Colchester also accumulated wealth. It is perhaps surprising that it has left us so few monuments. The eight churches within the walls all received substantial additions, though none emerged as a cathedral in waiting; we do not talk in Colchester of 'wool churches'. The Norman Moot Hall was transformed by several timber additions which engulfed its stone core. Most of the best buildings were domestic, multi-storeyed and jettied, but these have disappeared under more recent commercial pressure. The *Red Lion Inn*, a shop-front added to a house built in High Street in 1482 and 1501 by the powerful Dukes of Norfolk, is a rare survivor.

The tenth largest town was also quite slow to advance civic responsibilities. It was 1372 before Colchester moved beyond its governance by two bailiffs, with the sporadic help of 'under bailiffs'. In that year a new constitution created two new finance officers, receivers, later called chamberlains, to receive all the borough's

income. They, along with the two bailiffs, were to be elected by a council of 24 made up of 20 burgesses, chosen by one representative from each of four wards, plus those four men. The 24 then elected eight more men as auditors (soon to be called aldermen), who, with the

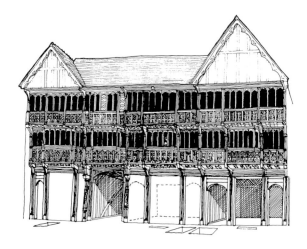

47 A reconstruction of the original appearance of the present *Red Lion Inn*, based on the research of David Stenning, showing the lavish display of carved wood it contained.

48 Medieval East Street was the smart end of Colchester. The Victorian artist, Major Bale, caught its lines of timbered buildings (looking east) before modern additions appeared.

bailiffs, would audit the annual accounts, after they had been drawn up by the receivers.

This, to our eyes, rather closed procedure served the town well and gave responsibility to a wide range of those citizens who, in a very different age, were both able and willing to accept it. In due course, an enlarged council became a somewhat self-perpetuating body, but was always subject to a great deal of public scrutiny. Scarlet robes and civic ceremony followed, though the town did not adopt the office of mayor as most large towns did. The greater merchants readily accepted the burden of repeated appointment. Thus Thomas Christmas and Thomas Christmas, father and son, together served the town as bailiff 19 times. From 1283 Colchester regularly sent two burgesses to Parliament.

Only burgesses could trade in the town or take part in borough government, election to that office being secured by inheritance, by completing an apprenticeship in the town or by payment of a lump sum. It is a measure of the value of burgess status that the lump sum grew considerably over time. Civic responsibility included two weekly law courts: a Monday court, and a 'foreign' court on Thursdays for 'foreigners' (i.e. non-burgesses). The survival from 1311 of many court records provides fascinating insights into that distant world. Rising commercial maturity is marked by a tenfold increase in small debt cases, often based on word-of-mouth agreements, reflecting a community struggling to find the credit which the expanding cloth industry required. By-laws protected the borough's interests in its own trade, as well as prosecuting those who dumped offal in the open street, purchased fish illegally before it reached the Hythe or rearranged the face of a Dutchman in a tavern on a Saturday night.

If Colchester's governance was parochial, this was in part because it was not owned or dominated by a powerful great lord. The latter might have given us the grand buildings we lack, but it might also have frustrated the honest endeavour which kept Colchester a successful, no-nonsense industrial town for several centuries. Such an achievement should not be understated. Nor were its wiser men lacking friends at court. Charters were renewed, along with privileges, and there can be no better footnote to this chapter than the fates of John, Lord FitzWalter and Lionel de Bradenham.

In 1351 FitzWalter was found guilty of all his Colchester crimes and his estates were confiscated by the Crown. After a spell in the Tower of London, he received a royal pardon on condition that he purchased his own estates back from the Crown, a process which took him the rest of his life. Lionel de Bradenham came before the Court of King's

49 A carefully restored 15th-century building in West Stockwell Street.

Bench in 1364 for his siege of Colchester. Four days after his arrest in Colchester he escaped, seeking sanctuary in the church of the Grey Friars. Surrendering as a felon, he was duly found guilty and granted a royal pardon on condition that he too paid an immense fine. It cost him his estate.

We have already noted that the town's parallel conflict with St John's Abbey was institutional not religious, and we cannot leave the turbulent and dangerous medieval world without recording its deep communal piety. If there was a world in which all men shared it was Christendom. Churches were enlarged and clergy paid only because congregations and patrons funded them. Colchester's grandest buildings were, appropriately, its priory and abbey churches to which were added, in the 13th century, two friaries. The Crouched (i.e.

Crossed) Friars (from which Crouch Street takes its name) had a chapel and a hospital; the Grey Friars on East Hill, where Lionel de Bradenham had sheltered, occupied a large block between the town wall and the Castle Bailey. The personal piety of wealthy men is reflected in the establishment of at least 27 chantries, most for a designated number of years, where priests were paid to pray for the departed soul of their patron. For the less wealthy, obits (prayers said on the anniversary of a death) were more popular. Feast days and religious festivals punctuated the Colchester year; mystery plays were performed.

The town notably sustained the cult of St Helena. Her image appeared on the borough seal, and Henry V's illuminated reissue of the borough charter in 1413, which may have been prepared in St John's Abbey, carries the

prototype of the borough arms, an elaborate allegory on the deeds of St Helena. Then there was the Guild of St Helena, established and sustained by the town's wealthiest merchants, endowed with land and rents, with its own priest, vestments and plate. By 1490 it was associated with the Chapel of St Cross in Crouch Street and included in its members up to 87 leading local figures, including gentry from the surrounding area, forming the very epitome of a 20th-century Rotary Club. For lesser citizens almost every parish had at least one guild. Dedications included the Jesus Mass, St Ann, St Barbara, St Crispin and St Crispian (the patron saints of cobblers). The Crouched Friars sold 'pardons', identical to those which so enraged Martin Luther, to finance their hospital. Every parish church had at least a light dedicated to the Virgin Mary. Even religious radicalism was evidence of religious strength. On the eve of what we call the Reformation the Catholic faith remained active, engaged and universal in the parish life of Colchester.

50 The earliest version of the borough's coat of arms appears in the decorated initial H of the 1413 charter issued to the town by Henry V. St Helena holds the cross which her son, Constantine the Great, grasps. Below left, the coat of arms consists of a cross with nails sustaining three crowns, commemorating the legend of St Helena who found the true cross of Christ (it miraculously burst into life) as well as the tombs of 'the Three Kings'.

51 John Driver, Prior of the Crouched Friars, issued this 1523 pardon (seen by Protestants as selling the forgiveness of sins) to raise money for the hospital in Crouch Street. The pardon was found in the binding of a book in Chichester Cathedral, hence the trimmed side and base.

Five

The Godly Town
1525-1640

The profound long-term consequences of Henry VIII's break with Rome, in order to divorce his wife, framed Colchester's history over the next 100 years. Political, social, and even economic change hinged on the role of religion in the community; but a godly town was not necessarily a quiet town. Religious tension, indeed religious conflict, was one legacy of the schism, and this had deep roots in Colchester.

A century before the Reformation there had been local support for those early Protestants, the Lollards, whose opposition to the Papacy and condemnation of Catholic 'superstition' was based on their reading of the Bible in English. In Colchester, where literacy levels were high, Lollards had 'many English books' which 'they read day and night'. In 1429 one of their number, a tailor named William Chiveling, was burnt at the stake outside Colchester Castle. Also executed was John Abraham, a Colchester shoemaker, who was 'keeping and holding schools of heresy'. Lollards were still active in the district in 1500, when William Sweeting, a Lollard teacher, instructed James Brewster, a Colchester carpenter, while they were in the field tending livestock. Both were burnt at Smithfield, London, in 1511.

Such men came from relatively modest backgrounds but investigations by the Bishop of London in 1528-9 showed not only significant support for Lollardy in the Colchester district, but support among the families of leading aldermen. Up to forty local people were named,

52 The burning of the Colchester Lollards, William Sweeting and James Brewster, at Smithfield in 1511.

most of whom were quick to back down from the terrible consequences of continued heresy.

As a port close to the Low Countries, Colchester was used to smuggle in Tyndale's illegal New Testament and other protestant literature, hidden in bales of cloth, often en route for London. Prompted by tracts produced by Martin Luther, there was a growing readiness in Colchester to criticise clerical shortcomings.

53   Thomas Audley as Lord Chancellor.

54   The youthful Richard Rich (based on a drawing by Holbein).

Charges of violent behaviour and sexual misconduct, normally the province of church courts, were brought against several Colchester priests in the borough courts. A 1528 entry in the borough records talks casually of 'priests and other knaves'.

For all these reasons Colchester was likely to support the dramatic changes begun by the King's wish to divorce Catherine of Aragon and marry Anne Boleyn. Though Protestantism was at first the religion of a minority, in Colchester it had influential support. The town's leaders were also well advised by a man at the eye of the storm. Thomas Audley of Earl's Colne, for 18 years town clerk of Colchester, rose to become Speaker of the House of Commons and later Lord Chancellor, as Henry VIII moved first to become supreme head of the English Church and then to suppress the monasteries. Through these momentous years Audley retained his house in Head Street, Colchester, continued to

buy and sell land in the district and remained a friend and adviser of Colchester.

Audley in turn was joined by Richard Rich, another young lawyer, who first represented Colchester in Parliament, later became the town's recorder, and later still followed Audley to the post of Lord Chancellor. These two men were key figures in the devising of royal strategy. Perhaps the most important political reality of Tudor Colchester was its friends in high places. Increasingly the town chose as its M.P.s not its own aldermen, but lawyers and county gentry building a parliamentary career, often looking to the powerful earls of Oxford (of Hedingham Castle) as their patron. The position of Colchester Recorder, the town's chief legal officer, was later held by such prominent statesmen as Sir Thomas Heneage and Sir Francis Walsingham.

Meanwhile in 1529, on the eve of the Reformation Parliament, all seemed normal in

55 The late medieval gate to St John's Abbey survived the dissolution of the monasteries to become the entrance to the Lucas house. This early photograph taken on St John's Green pre-dates the Victorian 'restoration' of the gateway.

the town. The abbot of St John's Abbey, before taking his seat in the House of Lords, sued John Thomson of Colchester for allowing his animals to stray into the abbey's herb garden. Just ten years later, the abbot's successor, William Marshall (also called Beche) was dragged on a hurdle through the streets of Colchester, then hanged and disembowelled outside the main gate of the town, for failing to hand over his abbey to the King. We can well imagine how this gruesome public spectacle bought home to ordinary townsfolk the reality of royal supremacy.

The suppression of the Grey Friars, the Crossed Friars, St Botolph's and St John's had other long-term consequences for Colchester, though there is little evidence that their closure was unpopular. Indeed, St John's Abbey had long been the town's great institutional rival. For the monks, canons and friars, fewer than fifty in number, new opportunities beckoned, often as curates of local churches. Thomas Turnour, the

last prior of St Botolph's and a willing supporter of royal supremacy, became rector of Great Wigborough. The poor of Colchester, who had benefited from monastic charity, were less fortunate. Local parishes suffered too. No longer able to look to the monasteries and chantries for clergy, they scarcely had the resources to pay a curate. All but three of Colchester's parishes had had their clergy appointed by the abbey and the priory. Now they passed into gentry hands. Thomas Audley in particular was not always successful when using his new powers to appoint clergy.

The extensive monastic estates provided the largest market in land since the Norman Conquest and several local families benefited. St John's was the great prize. Thomas Audley hoped, but failed, to secure it. In the event it served to launch three new gentry families: the Audleys; the Jobsons (or Jopsons), an old Colchester family; and the Lucases, founded by John Lucas, another Colchester town clerk, who

56   The burning of John Lawrence, seated in a chair. Note the children and crowd chanting.

rebuilt St John's Abbey as a substantial gentry mansion. The borough also gained, acquiring by charter the extensive Kingswood Heath, formerly royal land. Finally, as a sweetener for supporting royal supremacy and conducting the trial of Abbot Marshall, the borough was granted the income from Colchester's two largest chantries to fund the establishment of a grammar school. The post of master was briefly held by Samuel Harsnett (originally Halsnoth), son of a St Botolph's baker, who later became Archbishop of York.

In terms of theology Henry's Reformation was distinctly conservative and the borough of Colchester followed his middle way. Court records show the continued suppression of more radical protestant views when expressed by the humbler classes. Whatever they might think themselves, leading aldermen, advised from Westminster, hastened to stay in line. Their time came with Henry's successor Edward VI, the boy king, whose government took a more radical religious path. Now we begin to see real change in Colchester churches: services conducted in English; images and

altars removed; church plate sold and medieval paintings covered up as church walls were whitewashed and windows fitted with plain glass. Prayers for the dead ceased as chantry and guild lands were sold. It is noticeable that Colchester was more ready to do this than more traditional towns like Oxford and York, where such change was only introduced grudgingly over a period of many years. The study of surviving wills also shows leading Colchester families as being ready to adopt more extreme forms of protestant dedication.

Trial by Fire

In 1553 the sickly King Edward died to be succeeded by his Catholic sister Mary. Efforts to supplant her with the Protestant Lady Jane Grey involved two of Colchester's 'men at court', Sir Francis Jobson and John Lucas. Colchester's leaders, however, welcomed Mary to Colchester as she made her way to London, presenting her with a silver cup and £20 in gold. For all their reformist beliefs the burgesses recognised a legitimate Tudor monarch. Their very independence as a corporation rested on royal charters. Jobson and Lucas, though both initially imprisoned, were soon pardoned. The Queen meanwhile made clear her intention of returning the English Church to the care of Rome.

In January 1554 her Privy Council summoned Colchester's two bailiffs and two leading aldermen to appear before them in London. All four were men with firm Protestant views. We can only surmise what was said and what they replied. A month later the men of Kent rose in rebellion against Mary's proposed marriage with the Catholic Philip of Spain. They were harshly put down.

Colchester's leaders, we can conclude, had undertaken to be circumspect and law-abiding, but they could not answer for the passionate Protestant views which had now spread deep and wide among ordinary people. Colchester's inns became the meeting place for believers from as far off as Cambridgeshire. The *King's Head*, in Head Street, once Thomas Audley's town house, became home to the Family of Love, a Dutch sect, of 'many strange opinions'. Leading London Protestants like Master John Pullen (or Pulleyne) instructed the faithful there until, like other prominent preachers, he fled to Geneva. Recalling these times years later, Foxe in his *Book of Martyrs* declared:

> The ancient and famous city of Colchester, in the troublesome time of Queen Mary ... for the earnest profession of the gospel became like unto the city upon a hill, and as a candle upon a candlestick gave light to all those who ... came to confer there from divers places of the realm. And repairing to common inns had by night their Christian exercises.

Such activity cannot have escaped the attention of Edmund Bonner, the restored Catholic Bishop of London, whose pursuit of heretics intensified in 1556. Aided by such establishment figures as Lord Richard Rich, Colchester's former recorder, the public burnings began. From the outset the authorities sought to target 'determined heretics', some of whom seemed to embrace martyrdom. At a less sensational level, symbolic submissions were secured. One of Colchester's two bailiffs, Thomas Dybner, was summoned before the Privy Council at Hampton Court where he agreed to confess his religious offences in two Colchester parish churches. These confessions had to be witnessed by 'some of the chiefest and most honest of the town'. Thus was Colchester's leadership, unwilling to die for their beliefs, brought into line.

The first to die in Colchester was John Lawrence, his legs so injured by prison irons that he was burnt seated in a chair. As Lawrence, a former friar, exhorted the crowd, children placed at the front chanted, 'Lord strengthen thy servant and keep thy promises'. That these horrific scenes were counter-productive became clear as the burnings intensified. In

August 1557 six Colchester residents, three men and three women, were led from the Moot Hall, soon after dawn, to stakes piled with faggots outside the town walls. In the still morning air a crowd numbered in thousands had gathered. The six knelt to pray but were interrupted by Alderman Clere, a member of a prominent Protestant family and one of the two bailiffs hauled before the Privy Council at the start of the reign. He, like other aldermen, was required to conduct the day's events. Elizabeth Folkes, one of the condemned, was a servant of Clere's uncle. She pulled off her petticoat and tried to give it to her mother, who came to kiss her at the stake. Again, the alderman intervened. Such painful, personal detail would be remembered for decades to come. As the condemned exhorted the crowd to stand firm in their faith, the crowd in turn shouted encouragement as the flames were lit. Later that day another large crowd attended as two men and two women were burnt alive at a site in Castle Yard.

That two aldermen proved remarkably ready to help hunt down heretics was a fact never forgotten in the town, though most of Colchester's leaders seem to have done their best to limit the persecution. It also needs to be remembered that many Colchester citizens still had faith in Catholic practices and resented the changes thrust upon them in the past 20 years. The town, like the nation, faced division within itself. The death of Queen Mary in 1558 ended three of the most difficult years in Colchester's history. In just 30 months some 70 humble Essex citizens, men and women, young and old, had died in terrible public fashion. Most were from North-East Essex, with 16 from Colchester itself, a higher proportion than any other region in England.

Because Mary's reign was short and Elizabeth I's was long, England emerged a Protestant nation. Indeed, English Protestantism became a kind of English nationalism. The new

57 A group of Colchester Protestants being led bound to London: an illustration from Foxe's *Book of Martyrs*.

Queen was never more popular than when resisting the Spanish Armada (against which Colchester supplied one ship), an invasion launched by Mary's former husband, Philip of Spain. The Protestantism which Elizabeth I restored suited the godly of Colchester. At the first election after her accession three prominent Protestants were elected aldermen, replacing the most active heretic hunters. Other elections to the Common Council consolidated the hold of a reformist group. At the same time Master John Pullen returned from Geneva, where he had served under John Knox helping translate the Geneva Bible, to become Archdeacon of Colchester. Significantly and most unusually,

this Calvinist preacher was promptly made a freeman of Colchester.

Protestantism, with its emphasis on preaching rather than priests, called for a resident, educated clergy. Colchester had neither. Pullen's survey revealed that of Colchester's 14 parishes only the village of Mile End had a resident parson – and he soon became rector of Holy Trinity and curate at Berechurch as well. Holding several parishes in this manner became common as prolonged inflation rendered Colchester's modest church stipends too small to live on, particularly now that clergy might be married. Efforts to combine certain poor parishes came to nothing. Several churches in consequence

Briant hedd for adultrye
vd Alyce Samforde
vyddowe

Thomas ffawne for comittinge of
fornicacion vd helen markam

58-9 Surviving placards placed round offenders'
necks in the 1580s to record their moral
misdemeanours. They read: 'Briant Hedd for adultery
with Alice Samforde, widow' and 'Thomas Faune for
committing of fornication with Helen Markam'.

had a vacancy or made do with a curate. The
rector of St Leonard's, a Catholic, had been
excommunicated; the rector of St Mary's was
in prison for debt; the vicar of Lexden had not
been seen for 12 years. Even when appointed,
clergy might lack a Protestant education or be
unable to offer a preaching ministry. It was to
be 40 years before Colchester had a university-
educated clergy.

Into this spiritual vacuum stepped the
Protestant aldermen of Colchester, united by
family, a shared belief and long years in office,
ready to embrace the Genevan model of godly
magistrates promoting a godly community. In
1562 the council drew up detailed regulations
about attendance at church. Two persons from
each parish were to monitor the streets every
Sunday to check for unacceptable behaviour,
such as 'playing at football'. One person from
each household was required to attend a learned
sermon every Friday. Before long the sermon
was followed by a systematic collection for
the poor.

Initially most sermons were preached by
Archdeacon Pullen but from 1564 the aldermen
and council hired, at their own expense, a
'Town Preacher', Master William Cole, an
Oxford graduate and a translator of the Geneva
Bible, recently returned from Antwerp. Cole
was followed by Dr Withers from Heidelberg
University and he by Nicholas Challoner
from Cambridge, whose appointment for the
handsome stipend of £40 a year was financed

not by voluntary subscription, but from borough
income.

Thus the regular sermon of the town
preacher became a civic event attended by
aldermen and councillors, held in St James's
or St Botolph's Church. All four preachers
were made freemen and citizens. Bailiffs,
aldermen and archdeacon also sat together on
special tribunals to investigate prostitution and
fornication. Those convicted of adultery could
find themselves paraded round the town in a
tumbrel, their offences written on a placard.
Others confessed in church. Alehouses were
regulated and drunkards placed in the stocks; the
moral offender even risked losing the right to
vote. Sacred and secular were thus intertwined;
Colchester was becoming a Puritan town.

Against this background, also in 1562, bailiff
Benjamin Clere (he of the 1557 burnings)
wrote to the Privy Council, at his colleagues'
request, for permission to bring to Colchester
some Flemish refugees 'banished for God's
Word', fleeing from persecution by Catholic
Spain, seeking the 'establishing of their church
in this town'. Making every allowance for
hidden agendas, it seems that religion rather
than economics fuelled this request, leading
to 55 Dutch settlers coming to Colchester
in 1565. Only in 1570, when a further 200
arrived, did the borough concede the Dutch
expertise 'in such sciences as are not usual
to us', to wit their skill in the production of
new lightweight cloths, usually called 'the new

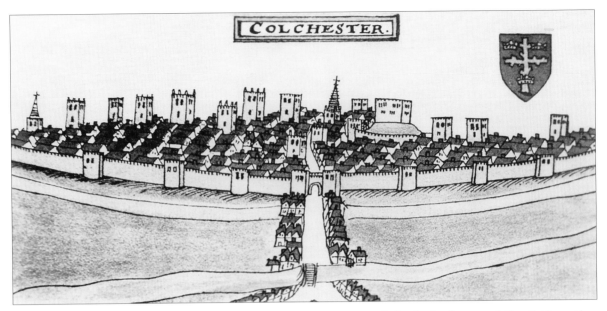

60 Colchester in 1588 seen from the east. This stylised picture includes, in the foreground, East Bridge with East Mill, East Street entering East Gate and leading up East Hill, the town walls and ditch stretching either side. Note the castle on the horizon on an earth mound with a curtain wall below; this may not be strictly accurate. It is equally unlikely that we can identify each church.

draperies', a skill which was to sustain the town for the next 150 years.

Economic Prosperity

Colchester's economy was already very buoyant. It had weathered better than most the erosion of population that regular outbreaks of plague had caused in the 15th century. In 1525 Colchester had perhaps been the ninth town in the kingdom in terms of taxable wealth. Its success rested on four functions: its importance as a market; its role as an administrative centre; its port facilities; and its dominant cloth trade. Let us look at each in turn.

Colchester's main market was held three times a week, stretching the full length of its broad High Street. Specialist activities like the wool market were held on other days. Though small changes occurred, the big picture was one in which cleaner goods sold at the western end of High Street, more smelly and perishable items being found as one travelled east to St Nicholas Church. At the junction with North Hill stood

the Red Row, outside which grain changed hands. Opposite the Moot Hall were stalls selling butter, but here too a large fruit and poultry market was built in 1590. Beyond the Moot Hall were a cloth market and a large area for selling leather goods. Beyond St Runwald's Church a long butchers' shambles extended eastwards. Outside the *Red Lion Inn* fish was sold. Here too was an extensive vegetable mart, market gardening being a flourishing new trade, learnt from the Dutch. Colchester merchants sold from their own houses, stalls or workshops (from which glass-fronted 'shops' evolved); countryfolk would have a 'standing', selling from baskets or goods at their feet. Nor was this all. A specialist fish market was held at the Hythe and goods were also sold at several points on North Hill.

In addition Colchester held three annual fairs. The midsummer fair on St John's Green, formerly held by St John's Abbey, had now passed to the lord of the manor of West Donyland, but was supervised by the borough and formally visited by the bailiffs and aldermen.

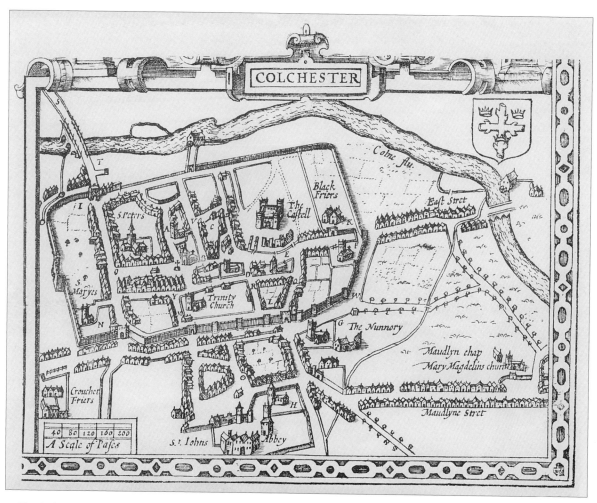

61 A far more accurate view of Colchester can be found in Speed's map of 1610. Among its many interesting features are the castle, the Lucas house at St John's Abbey, the correct number of bastions in the walls, the watermills, wells and water courses, and the built-up area of the town, essentially medieval, which did not significantly change until Victorian times.

Goods from a wide distance changed hands as did horses and other livestock. A second fair was held on Mary Magdalen Green on 21 and 22 July, its profits going to the master of the hospital there. But the town's great fair was the St Dennis Fair held for eight days in early October, extending from the top of High Street all the way to East Gate, taking in the large Bury Field running from East Street to the walls of St Botolph's. Specialist craftsmen from all over the country arrived, many sleeping in a shelter above their stall. In 1562 fletchers, bowyers, saddlers, soapers, tanners, glovers, shoemakers, blacksmiths, rope-makers, haberdashers, linen-drapers, hosiers, upholsterers, mercers, grocers, goldsmiths, pewterers, brasiers, ironmongers, nailers, turners, basket-makers, salters and whitesmiths were among those listed paying dues. Their pockets full of harvest money, people from a very wide area would come to purchase items not normally available, even in Colchester's market.

This major event was supervised by borough officials, as were the more routine weekly markets. Dues were collected (the contract was farmed out) and complex by-laws adopted to uphold standards, to protect the rights of resident freemen and control and restrict the activities of 'foreign' tradesmen. Wool, for example, was often bought and sold in inns, to avoid market regulations. This had to be resisted. Appropriately in 1578 the godly magistrates decreed that no trading – and no merrymaking – should take place on the Sunday of the St Dennis Fair.

Colchester was unusual, considering its size, in not being a county town, though its castle did house the county gaol. Assizes and Quarter Sessions and the business they generated all went to Chelmsford. Colchester did, however, stand at an important crossroad. The main road from London up the east coast via Ipswich ran down High Street and through East Gate. This was also the gateway to the Tendring Hundred, a considerable rural hinterland which looked towards Colchester. Head Street-North Hill provided the main river crossing to the important Stour Valley cloth industry. From the west came Stane Street via other major cloth centres at Coggeshall and Braintree. For all these reasons Colchester's inns were full, its markets busy and its jurisdiction respected. It was a town with lawyers.

Nationally, Colchester was not a major port: half the size of Ipswich and barely in the top twenty. Its shallow tidal channel guaranteed that. However, the Hythe was still a major source of business. Only the cloth trade provided more employment. Fish were a major source of cheap food, while the oyster fishery rose to some importance during the Elizabethan years. Colchester's men at court like Sir Francis Walsingham were rewarded with *cartloads* of oysters sent down to London. While much of Colchester's cloth trade was controlled from London, this still provided a good deal of coastal transport. And not only cloth. Butter, cheese, grain, leather and faggots went to the capital, and in return dyestuff, soap, oil and luxury goods were joined by fuller's earth from Kent. A growing volume of 'sea coal' and salt came down from Tyneside, quantities of grain going back in return. As the new draperies began to be exported to the Low Countries, often in foreign ships, back came specialist cargoes of potash, spices, linens and groceries transported on to London. Though never in the big league, a few Colchester ships still went to ports in France, Germany and even Spain. Adequate records have not survived, but trade at the Hythe expanded throughout the century. Colchester's 42 licensed vessels of 1582 with a combined weight of 1,246 tons imply a good deal of fishing and small cargo work.

The English cloth trade was not flourishing in the early 16th century. Such growth as there was seems to have taken place in rural areas: notably, in Colchester's case, in the Stour Valley, in Lavenham, Coggeshall, Dedham. Colchester's continued prosperity was sustained as much by diversity as specialisation, by its market and port, its food and drink trades, its leather-working skills. Hence the importance of the Flemings and their new draperies for an emphatic renewal of the cloth industry. As more immigrants arrived, the Dutch became a community within a community: 1,291 citizens in a population of 5-6,000 by 1586. The key to their success was a new generation of light, relatively cheap cloths, generally called bays and says, the market for which, particularly in southern Europe, was far more buoyant than for the old Colchester russets.

The Dutch had a secret weapon – quality control. The upper floor of the old Red Row at the top of High Street, overlooking St Peter's Churchyard, became the Dutch Bay Hall. Here all bays and says were taken for inspection by the Governors, before sealing with decorated lead seals. Such was the reputation this cloth

acquired and the strictness with which it was
controlled that the very presence of the seal
was enough to satisfy a customer. One notable
consequence was the manufacture of fake
Colchester seals in the back streets of London.
Despite occasional disputes with English
weavers, the Dutch Company's privileges were
regularly upheld throughout the 17th century.
This liberal approach by the corporation paid
handsome dividends. The Dutch community
in Halstead opted to return to Colchester,
recognising these advantages.

In Colchester the Dutch sustained their
own minister, Theodorus van den Berghe,
whose bilingualism was invaluable. For a
while they worshipped in All Saints Church,
before erecting their own church (in modern
Church Street), the timbers sent over from the
Netherlands cut and ready to be assembled.
The population grew as the bay trade came to
dominate the town's economy. By the 1620s
Colchester's head count had reached 11,000,
perhaps forty per cent of whom lived by the
cloth trade. For the first time in its history
Colchester was a major industrial town and
back among the 'top ten' in England.

There were, of course, trade fluctuations
and bad years. The life of a weaver could be
hard. Real hunger could threaten the constantly
changing ranks of the poor, as late Elizabethan
England struggled to cope with an expanding
population and a mobile underclass of 'sturdy
beggars'. Colchester exhibited a similar anxiety
to care for the widow and orphan but to
remove the feckless and dangerous; to stem
the tide of unwanted immigrants. The informal
appeals for money after the Friday sermon
became more structured. Begging was banned.
Local charities were used to set the poor to
work in a 'poorhouse'. As in London, a tax
based on property was levied in each parish
to sustain its resident poor. Colchester's godly
corporation had invented household rates.
Codified by the government in the 1601 Poor

62 A highly decorated lead seal placed on
Colchester cloth showing, once again, Colchester
Castle.

Law, it was a system which was to survive
for over 200 years. Colchester was not the
only large town doing this, but it was in the
vanguard of experiment.

By the time Queen Elizabeth died in 1603
(cared for by her physician William Gilberd,
another noted Colcestrian, more famous today
for his experiments with electro-magnetism),
Colchester was a fully Protestant town.
Religious diversity, however, was growing.
Within the shelter of great houses like Lady
Audley's at Berechurch, the Catholic faith
lived on. But a growing number of advanced
Protestants not only rejected all ceremony
(such as the clergy wearing a surplice), but
also embraced the Presbyterian view that
bishops were unnecessary; that each church
congregation could govern itself. A group of
mainly Cambridge-educated clergy met to
discuss these views at the important Dedham
Classis.

From the 1580s Archbishop Whitgift's drive
to enforce clerical conformity caused conflict
with this group. George Northey, Colchester's

63 Dr William Gilberd, drawn from a lost portrait.

64 Dr John Bastwick, the outspoken critic of all that Archbishops Laud and Harsnett believed in.

town preacher, was for a period suspended and imprisoned. Divisions even occurred within the once united borough aldermen. It is also clear that, in a world where religious persuasion was a matter of personal, not communal, commitment, a growing number of people were not particularly religious at all, yet upheld that right to express a view which Protestantism had encouraged. Colchester gained a reputation for aggressively upholding its rights. Thus when the new King's Direction to Preachers in 1622 caused dispute over the appointment of Colchester's town preacher, the bishop's commissary protested that the town 'will allow no minister but of their own choice'. Colchester got its way, but clashes with the Bishop of London led subsequent preachers to flee to Holland.

Conflict was therefore inevitable when Archbishop Laud was appointed by Charles I to enforce a more ceremonial church orthodoxy, an orthodoxy codified by the Archbishop of York, Samuel Harsnett, once master of the

town's grammar school. Laud's famous order to erect altar rails in all churches was obeyed by most Colchester clergy, some of whom held High Church views themselves, but it created outcry among advanced Protestants. They saw this as counter-revolution, part of a terrible possibility that England would be returned to 'Popery', if not to Roman rule. Colchester's town lecturer had his licence revoked and soon afterwards left for Puritan New England.

Once more Colchester produced its martyrs, notably Dr John Bastwick, opponent of the Rev. Thomas Newcomen, the leading Laudian enforcer in the town. Summoned before the King's High Commission in London, Bastwick's outspoken writing led to a fine, two imprisonments and the removal of his ears in the pillory. Charles I had now dispensed with Parliament, initiating his 11-year period of 'Personal Rule'. Bastwick's 'martyrdom' caused rumblings in London as England stumbled towards political crisis.

Six

From Civil War to Commercial Crisis
1640-1720

The conflict between King and Parliament which led to the Civil War, a war in which the Parliamentary army came to rule England, to execute King Charles and to appoint Oliver Cromwell as Lord Protector in his place, had profound consequences for Colchester. Not only did civil war induce all but the poorest to hold political views, but Colchester's size, closeness to London, volatile cloth trade and religious radicalism, gave it strategic significance as the political nation slid towards conflict.

In 1640 the King's fateful decision to impose an English Prayer Book on Scotland led directly to war, forcing the recall of Parliament after an absence of 11 years. Parliament put on trial and then executed the King's chief minister, Strafford, imprisoned Archbishop Laud and abolished all non-Parliamentary taxation. As rebellion erupted in Ireland, Charles I made the fatal mistake of going to the House of Commons to attempt to arrest five leading opponents. With growing unrest in the capital, the King left London. Government censorship collapsed and a war of words began. Pamphlets printed in London rapidly reached Colchester.

65 The arrival of the Catholic Queen Mother, Marie de Medici, in Colchester East Street in 1638 to stay with Sir John Lucas. By a fine irony John Furley, the mayor presenting her with a silver cup, was an advanced Protestant. The artist may have devised his drawing from the 1610 Speed map.

66 A contemporary (but imaginative) view, taken from Royalist propaganda, of the 1642 assault on Sir John Lucas's house.

67 Sir Harbottle Grimston, M.P. for Colchester, would eventually become Speaker of the House of Commons.

By the summer of 1642 both King and Parliament were seeking to raise a national army to suppress the Irish rebellion. Which of the two authorities were local officials supposed to obey? In Essex, widespread Puritan sympathies, underpinned by several of the leading county families, ensured a greater support for the Parliamentary cause. By August some five hundred Parliamentary volunteers, financed in part by the town, were stationed at Colchester. But not all leading families supported such action.

In Colchester a special position was held by the Lucas family and its head, Sir John Lucas. As owners of St John's Abbey, which had been converted into their private house, the Lucases seem to have inherited the long-running conflict with the corporation and the citizens of Colchester which had once dogged the Abbey. 'Nor will men serve him, though he were hanged at his gate,' it was said of John Lucas's grandfather. A series of disputes over

enclosure of common lands, woodland theft and water pipes laid across Lucas land made Sir John Lucas equally unpopular. Lucas moreover took an exaggerated view of his honour as a gentleman, was outspoken in his support of royal policy and held conservative religious views which Puritans regarded as 'Popish.' He appointed as his chaplain the Rev. Thomas Newcomen, the hated enforcer in Colchester of Archbishop Laud's High Church policies.

In August 1642 rumour ran round Colchester that Lucas was assembling arms and troops to ride to the King's cause. Conscious of widespread popular opposition, the mayor of Colchester put a watch on St John's Abbey. On the night of 22 August (the very day King Charles raised his standard of war in Nottingham), as Sir John Lucas sought to leave by his back gate, the alarm was raised and a crowd numbered in thousands—men, women and children—besieged the house. A crowd so large may have been assembled from the surrounding district, and the extent to which the violence which followed was sustained by leading members of Colchester's 'godly' elite is not clear.

At dawn the crowd broke into the Abbey, and manhandled Lucas, his wife and his mother. They and Thomas Newcomen, whom the crowd set upon and nearly killed, were taken by the mayor to the Moot Hall, and ghosted to London the next day by the town's M.P., Sir Harbottle Grimston, who had rushed back to help the mayor. Arms were found in St John's Abbey, though not on the scale implied, and the place was systematically ransacked. Even the family tombs in St Giles's Church were broken into and desecrated. The mob went on to attack the houses of Sir Henry Audley at Berechurch and the Countess Rivers at St Osyth, both prominent Catholic households. Over the following days similar crowd violence, directed against Catholic or High Church family homes, occurred throughout the cloth-making area of the Stour Valley. Denounced in Royalist 'newsbooks', these events served to encourage many gentry families to join the King's cause. Conversely, Colchester's robust popular protestant radicalism was soon to be evident in the Eastern Association's New Model Army.

Over the next six years, as the Civil War ground on, Colchester contributed over £30,000 to sustain Parliamentarian armies. Not everyone approved. Complaints were made not only against billeted soldiers, but also against the 'heretics and schismatics' who held advanced religious views within the ranks. The election of a Royalist, John Shaw, as mayor in September 1647 suggests opinion among the freemen of Colchester was swinging against the army. A 'riotous and tumultuous assembly' against the billeting of soldiers led to the calling out of troops to restore order.

The new office of mayor (in place of two bailiffs) had begun in 1635 almost as a by-product of friction between the borough and the free burgesses over the enclosure of common land and the extent to which the town's charter encouraged oligarchy or permitted popular election. It is also probable that Charles I's government valued this opportunity to remind Colchester Corporation of the source of its power. The revised charter left Colchester more of an oligarchy, but mayors, at least, were annually elected. John Shaw did not last long, his election annulled by a troop of Parliamentary horse. His replacement refused to serve, so the mayor for 1647-8, William Cooke, was the third choice. Little did he realise what he was in for.

The Siege of Colchester

Late in the Civil War Colchester was sucked into conflict. With the King defeated and held on the Isle of Wight, a new Royalist army, led by Lord Goring, was formed in Kent. Failing to raise support in London it marched through Essex, arriving, 5,000-strong, at the gates of Colchester in June 1648. Among its experienced leaders was Sir Charles Lucas, brother of Sir John. The town gates were shut against him, but Royalist numbers were such that the mayor, reluctant to admit them himself, threw the keys over the walls.

The Royalists intended only a short stay to gather supplies and perhaps recruit among the town's population of poor weavers. Goring's army, however, had been closely tracked by Lord Fairfax and the New Model Army. Marching through the night, Fairfax arrived the next day and called on the town to surrender. Goring refused. A bloody battle fought to secure an entry at Headgate failed, forcing Fairfax to settle down to a siege. It lasted 11 weeks as Colchester's ancient walls saw military action for the last time. Slowly Fairfax tightened the noose round the town, building an extensive series of earthen forts, even bringing 40 heavy cannons from the Tower of London to batter

68 Sir Charles Lucas, effective leader of the Royalist side at the siege of his native Cochester, paid for his allegiances with his life.

69 A contemporary drawing of Sir Thomas Fairfax, Parliamentary leader at the Siege of Colchester.

Royalist strongpoints, several of which were placed in churches. In this way St Mary's, St Martin's, St Giles', St Botolph's and St John's Abbey were reduced to some ruin. Houses caught in crossfire were similarly damaged or destroyed as both sides sought to deny their opponents shelter. Inside the shrinking town deprivation and disease mounted, as food ran out among 4,000 troops and perhaps 10,000 civilians. Horses, dogs, cats, even rats, were eaten. The cloth trade ceased to function.

On 27 August the Royalists surrendered. Their two main military leaders, Sir Charles Lucas and Sir George Lisle, were shot by firing squad behind the castle; Goring was later spared execution by one vote in the House of Lords. Surviving Royalist soldiers were roughly treated, some taken as slaves to the West Indies. Within five months Charles I was beheaded. Colchester was held responsible for its siege and fined the huge sum of £12,000, half of which was met by the Dutch community, £2,000 of which was

returned for helping the poor. Several wealthy citizens lost small fortunes. Parts of the town's walls were demolished; several hundred houses lay damaged or destroyed, particularly in the suburbs. Rebuilding began, but scars remained for a long time. As late as 1722 Daniel Defoe wrote that the town 'still mourns in the ruins of a civil war' with its 'battered walls … and ruined churches'.

As the rule of Oliver Cromwell extended, Colchester remained surly. The 'Cromwellian' group of aldermen led by Henry Barrington were ousted in the 1650s by the free burgesses, resulting in a purge of all dissidents, conducted by Cromwell's major-general, Hezikiah Haynes. A new charter in 1656 excluded the freemen from borough government and troops were quartered in the town amid talk of Colchester being seized on behalf of Charles II. Appropriately it fell to Sir Harbottle Grimston, for so long the town's M.P., now elevated to Speaker of the House of Commons, to

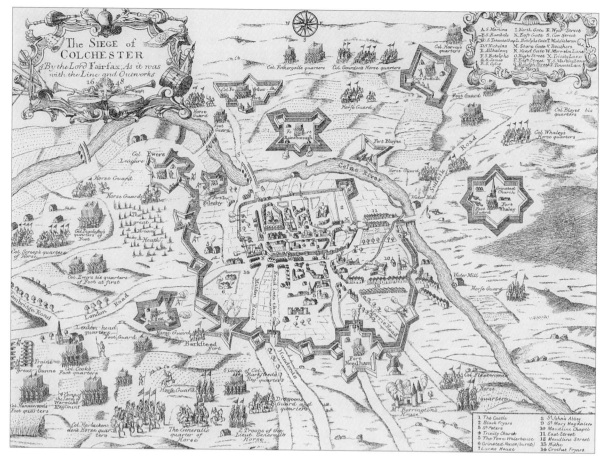

70 Map showing the Parliamentary batteries which gradually encircled Colchester. The artist may have exaggerated their robustness.

71 This contemporary picture of the Siege of Colchester stresses the role of artillery (note the telescope) and the supplies the Royalists secured on the river. Death stands on the right.

welcome Charles II on his return as King after the death of Cromwell. Counter-purges of Colchester Corporation in 1660 and 1662 followed the restoration of monarchy. Most senior Cromwellians were removed, replaced by almost a new generation of aldermen. A new charter restored most of the provisions of 1635.

If the siege and its aftermath left deep damage on the psyche of the town, ever visible in its ruined churches, a greater

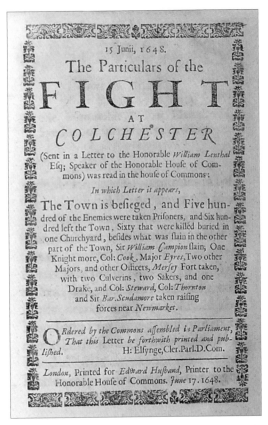

72 The Siege of Colchester was also a war of words. Both sides sought, with pamphlets like this, to claim legitimacy.

trauma came with the last great outbreak of bubonic plague in England in 1665-6. Usually referred to as the 'Great Plague of London', it wreaked greater proportionate damage in North Essex. Indeed, it has been claimed that Colchester suffered the heaviest infection-induced mortality of any provincial town since medieval times. Outbreaks of epidemic disease had been a recurring feature of Colchester during the Tudor and early Stuart period: in 1514, 1545, 1557-9, 1569-70, 1586-8, 1597, 1603-4, 1625-6, 1631 and 1651. Plague was the usual reason for these high death years, though cumulatively they represented less than 10 per cent of contemporary mortality. Infant death was by far the greater killer: perhaps only half of all children lived to the age of ten.

73 This Royalist pamphlet paints the executed Lucas and Lisle as martyrs. Lucas lies dying; Lisle says, 'Shoot rebels', and adds, 'your shot your shame, our fall our fame'.

The outbreak of 1665-6 was on an altogether different scale. Contemporary figures suggest 5,259 deaths between August 1665 and December 1666 in a population of perhaps 11,000. This may not, however, mean half the population. Deaths were highest in the summer months and the able-bodied dead would be rapidly replaced by migrants from the countryside. It is arguable that we are looking at two sets of mortality: death among the poor in the summer of 1665,

Burying the dead with a bell before them.   Searchers.

Carts full of dead to bury.

74 The Great Plague of 1665-6, graphically shown in these contemporary scenes of Searchers of the Plague organising mass burials, was more widespread in Colchester than in any other town.

followed by death among their replacements in 1666. This, however, cannot have reduced the sense of crisis, a crisis across the region, for mortality was almost as high in the cloth towns of Braintree and Bocking. Even London, absorbed in its own drama, took note. Samuel Pepys recorded in his diary that plague 'raged mightily' in Colchester and was expected 'to quite depopulate the place'. The cloth trade's output fell by about two-thirds. Parish organisation hardly survived, especially with the death of several clergy. Even for the elite, death stalked the streets: for a period in 1666 neither the mayor, nor many aldermen or councillors were present in the town. Two large pest houses were built and 'Searchers of the Plague', equipped with white wands, lived apart from their families, hunting infection and unburied corpses, consigning them to mass graves.

The gravity of Colchester's situation is marked by the support it received. Money collected in its own churches soon proved inadequate. Taxes were therefore levied on villages within five miles, then raised throughout adjacent hundreds, then taken from four more distant Essex hundreds and finally, on direct intervention from the King, raised by weekly collections in London churches, notwithstanding their own plague-related needs. In all £2,700 was raised for the relief of Colchester, a sum painstakingly dispensed among the poor by the authorities. For recover the town quickly did. It even raised £103 for the relief of Londoners after the Great Fire. As already noted, rural migrants quickly took up vacancies in the workforce and, as was the case after the siege, the cloth trade rapidly recovered, and in fact continued to expand. One community, however, could not be restored by in-migration. After 1666 the register of the Dutch church shows a sharp decline in both the community's size and activities.

It is worth recalling that throughout these crises Colchester was still among the ten largest towns in the kingdom. This was due solely to the cloth trade, to the specialist market in bays and says supervised from the Dutch Bay Hall. A trade established for nearly a century, involving both 'Dutch' and English merchants, made Colchester a rare example of a medieval cloth town which continued to flourish into the 18th century, though (as we shall see) only just. There was a price. Cloth was an industry built on cheap labour, subject to cyclical bouts of boom and depression. If England was at war with Spain the whole trade might stop. Baymakers found themselves with bays they were unable to sell and promptly ceased all production. A thousand weavers might be out of work and women spinners in surrounding villages felt a sharp reduction in their combined household earnings.

Colchester had, in consequence, a broad base in poverty. In 1674 over 60 per cent of the population was too poor to pay any hearth tax. In smaller cloth-weaving communities like Braintree the percentage was even higher. Colchester was, in John Evelyn's memorable phrase, both 'ragged and factious'. The regular whipping and expulsion of vagrants was matched by attempts to control alehouses and drunkenness. From 1622 four beadles were appointed to hunt out unlicensed beggars. In 1613 a new workhouse, significantly called a 'house of correction', was built in which to employ the poor. In times of dearth, such as 1630-1, when long-distance vagrancy was a real problem, the corporation actively intervened to acquire grain from afar or to prevent local grain leaving the town. Cheap fish was an important source of protein: the abundant local catches of sprats were known as 'weavers' beef'. The last quarter of the century seems to have left the town less plagued by poverty, yet we have no

significant public building to mark this last era when Colchester was a major English town.

The cloth trade appears to have become more capitalistic as the century progressed, with a steady decline in the number of small baymakers and independent weavers and a corresponding emphasis on capitalist clothiers employing waged labour, paid by the piece. The weavers in turn began to exert organised collective action. They even succeeded, by direct application to the Privy Council, in getting an unpopular baymaker imprisoned, until he made financial restitution, for 'paying' his workers in overpriced, unsold cloth. At the reputable end of the trade, it is noticeable that 75 per cent of Colchester apprentices (and this was true of all trades) were in-migrants, overwhelmingly from Essex and Suffolk. Colchester remained a magnet as a source of employment. In this way the body of free burgesses (who were entitled to vote) grew, representing between one quarter and one half of the male heads of household: 450 in 1619, 1,100 in 1704. Somehow the *George Hotel* in High Street accommodated 331 free burgesses for an election dinner in 1617, an obvious precursor of the later Colchester Oyster Feast. Indeed, it is a mark of Colchester's economic buoyancy that the 'fee' for the purchase of the freedom, necessary for anyone wishing to trade in the town, was raised to £10 in 1631 and now required the support of members of that trade. From 1654 it required the consent of the borough assembly too.

The Hythe remained a busy port. Exports of new draperies increased fourfold during the 17th century. London, and notably the Merchant Adventurers, now dominated the marketing of Colchester cloth, and bays formed a major part of a regular coastal traffic: 25,000 cloths in the year 1698-9. The poor state of the road to London was one reason, though this in turn was a reflection of overloaded wagons and a much increased traffic, notably of incoming raw wool. By sea came ever more Newcastle

75 A view of Colchester from the north in 1697 showing, on the skyline from the left, the old St Peter's Church, North Hill leading down to North Gate (see page 82), then the *Three Crowns Inn*, then the roofless St Mary's Church with, behind it, the windmill on Butt Road. On the slopes below, the long tenter frames are used to stretch and dry cloth after fulling. Far right is Balkerne Hill, flanked by the town wall.

coal and a range of specialist goods: Rhenish wine, Swedish iron, Dutch cheese, Norwegian deals and Danish pickled herrings. Grain and leather exports grew. Colchester had its own leather hall and the wealth of several local maltsters reflected a rising industry. Oysters were exported in prodigious quantities to France, and Colchester was noted for producing candied eryngo roots, an alleged aphrodisiac, a box of which was presented to the future James II on his visit to the town. In 1702 Colchester's port had 344 mariners and 34 registered vessels, weighing 3,675 tons.

Throughout a turbulent century the town's government proved equal to its task. The shortcomings of the tidal river received regular attention: in 1623 and 1698 Acts of Parliament were secured, enabling the corporation to raise tolls with which to widen, deepen and straighten the channel. Local economic activity was supervised to a remarkable extent. As well as collecting and spending poor rates, the assembly controlled wages, set the price of bread, appointed bakers' and butchers' wardens,

searchers of leather and overseers of the town land, notably the important half-yearly lands around the town where free burgesses might keep their livestock from August to February.

Trade disputes were usually settled in borough courts while the Dutch Bay Company was allowed freedom of action to control its trade. The town even ran its own lottery to support the poor, while the officers of the town's 16 parishes supervised the disbursements of an increasingly complex Poor Law. In 1698 an Act of Parliament established a central municipal workhouse, its inmates, many of them children, spinning wool for the cloth trade, the profits from their endeavours being distributed to the destitute.

As in all large towns, local government depended on the willingness of its substantial citizens, many from the cloth trade but also drapers, grocers, millers, general merchants and even master craftsmen, to serve in the three tiers of the Assembly, as the full council was called. At its base were 15 to 18 common councillors (numbers varied over time), from whom 15 to

76 Contemporary view of the self-proclaimed Witchfinder General Matthew Hopkins with two witches admitting those animals, or 'familiars', through whom they acted as evil spirits.

18 assistants were chosen, from whom 10 to 12 aldermen were elected. Mayors, chamberlains, coroners and J.P.s were largely chosen from the aldermen. After 1635 membership of the assembly was for life, unless improper conduct led to expulsion by a vote of the officers and the free burgesses. The assembly was thus a self-perpetuating and self-selecting body unless central government intervened, as it did after the Commonwealth and during the crisis which led to the overthrow of James II in 1689. In the former case, as we have seen, there were purges, as there had been after the siege. The latter case reflects Colchester's growing importance as a stronghold of religious Nonconformity, a process that had been ongoing for most of the century.

Even when Queen Elizabeth had died advanced Protestants, favouring the right of a congregation to govern themselves, had been in dispute with Colchester's town preacher. The town already housed an independent Dutch Calvinist church. Presbyterian views were increasingly held by such leading figures as the town's M.P., Harbottle Grimston, yet when, during the Cromwellian period, Presbyterianism governed the parish churches, most Colchester citizens favoured wholly independent congregations. The visiting diarist John Evelyn found Colchester 'swarming with sectaries' (sectarians). Baptist and Fifth Monarchy preachers toured the town and a large Quaker community was established. This often suffered attack for its outspoken views and its first active preacher, the youthful James Parnell, died while imprisoned in Colchester Castle. The mid-century was also noted for witchcraft accusations and trials. Victims of the self-styled Witchfinder General, Matthew Hopkins, were also held in the castle.

The restoration of the monarchy in 1660 saw a restoration of the Church of England to its former structure and doctrines. The 1662 Corporation Act required all borough office holders to take Anglican communion. A number of leading Colchester citizens would not do so. Two leading ministers, Owen Stockton, the Town Preacher, and Edward Warren of St Peter's, were unwilling to accept the required Act of Conformity, becoming leaders of what evolved into the Nonconformist congregation still active today in Lion Walk. Meetings were held in private houses and often in secret: the 1670s were not easy years for Nonconformity. Yet 170 adherents were recorded in the bishop's census of 1672, compared with two Roman Catholics and 1,891 conformists.

In this climate the new King, James II, a Catholic, sought, by granting religious toleration, to gain Nonconformist support against those Anglicans opposed to his own Roman Catholic faith. In 1684 and again in 1687, as part of a national move to control corporations, the King issued Colchester with new charters reducing the size of its assembly, giving himself the right to remove officials, but granting the right to non-Anglicans to become assembly members. For Colchester this had major consequences. Among the Nonconformists and their sympathisers were several leading families and a significant body of free burgesses. The new charter was followed by the establishment of special commissioners to gather evidence of the persecution of Nonconformists over the previous decade. In Colchester this was conducted with undoubted bitterness, borough officials being summoned to Chelmsford to meet with the regional commissioners. Labelled 'the Nonconformists' Revenge', the Commission undoubtedly hastened the determination of his opponents to replace James II with William of Orange and his wife, Mary. Faced with this coup, James II chose to flee the country, saving England from another potential civil war.

These events held long-term implications for Colchester. James II's Anglican opponents formed the core of the recently-named Tory Party, while Nonconformity found a home among their Whig counterparts. Britain's two-party system had been born with deep roots in provincial England. Over the next two centuries we should remember that in Colchester the age-old horizontal division between rich and poor might be matched, and rendered more complex, by a vertical division between Anglican and Nonconformist, between church and chapel, between Tories and Whigs (later Liberals). The battle for hearts and minds was not slow to follow. In 1710 a group of churchmen founded the Bluecoat School, which sustained the principles of the Church of England, followed soon afterwards by the Nonconformist Greencoat School.

Cloth trade crisis

In 1698 Colchester was visited by that adventurous traveller Celia Fiennes. She found the

77-8 These 1719 carvings of a Bluecoat boy and girl in uniform formerly stood outside the school in Culver Street.

town prosperous, its broad, well-kept streets complete with handsome sidewalks. Though most houses she thought old-fashioned, she noted the arrival of brick, as old properties upgraded their facades and what we term Georgian architecture appeared, deep gutters sustaining red-tiled roofs. By-laws now forbade the thatched roofs which had fed Royalist horses during the siege. 'The whole town', the traveller enthused, 'is employed in spinning, weaving, washing, drying and dressing their bays, in which they seem very industrious.' Visiting in 1722 Daniel Defoe formed a similar high opinion: 'the whole country employed in bay-making', which brought the town, he reckoned, £30,000 a week, the streets 'fair and beautiful', with 'an abundance of good and well-built houses'.

Such optimism, however, was for tourists. Between these two visits disturbing signs had appeared of a crisis in baymaking and with it the whole basis of Colchester's prolonged success. A high percentage of Colchester cloths now found their way to Portugal and Spain and their Latin American colonies. In 1700 the dying king of Spain left his Spanish dominions to a grandson of the French monarch. French

79 Bay tokens produced as small coin by Colchester baymakers to cope with a local shortage of currency.

influence in Spain rose, while Britain was sucked into fighting the War of Spanish Succession (1702-13) against France. Cloth exports to Spain halted and French manufacturers used this opportunity to penetrate the Spanish market with their own cheaper cloth. In 1707 Colchester's Dutch Bay Hall issued a by-law confining baymaking to those who had served an apprenticeship to an existing baymaker. Quotas were also placed on the output of bays. As a result, by 1715 the number of employers fell from 100 to 57; the industry was closing ranks. Even though the war ended, the Spanish market, increasingly penetrated by French products, was soon glutted.

A new lighter cloth was tried in Colchester, for which piece rates were reduced. One hundred weavers left the town. Discontent among the remainder erupted into the street. Seven hundred strong, they surrounded the Dutch Bay Hall, complaining of low piece rates, the use of unskilled labour, excessive fines for bad work and payment in cloth rather than money. A strike began. An armed mob broke into the gaol to release comrades imprisoned there by the mayor. They threatened to burn down the Dutch Bay Hall. The Bay Hall governors, for the moment, capitulated. The mayor called in the dragoons and appealed for help to London. The weavers had also petitioned the Privy Council, who upheld their complaints about payment in kind, but would not restore the old piece rates or rescind the 1707 apprenticeship clause. The weavers, still on strike, appealed to Parliament, who set up a Commons' Committee. Concluding that 'the poor weavers have been most grievously oppressed', they annulled the 1707 by-law, even though the cloth factors in London warned that restoring free entry to the trade would lead to over-production once more. The weavers had won a famous, but hollow, victory.

This most modern of disputes marks a turning point in Colchester's history. So early an example of industrial trade unionism proved helpless in the long term against market forces. Colchester had become over-dependent on one product, focused on too narrow a market, a market vulnerable to foreign competition and subject to the vagaries of international politics. This was not the first time this had happened to Colchester; nor was it to be the last.

Seven

The Long Decline
1720-1830

Throughout the 18th century Colchester's woollen industry, vulnerable to French and Yorkshire competition, to cheap cotton cloth and the disruption of war, continued its long decline. But it was a slow decline. Occasional booms, fuelled by the re-opening of the Spanish market after a war, usually produced new optimism, though always within a contracting trade. Cloth remained an important part of the town's economy until at least 1775, and only the long dislocation caused by the Napoleonic Wars between 1793 and 1815 marked the industry's true demise. By this date the town had been steadily transformed by an 'urban renaissance', common to provincial England, as the expanding middle ranks of society adopted a consumer lifestyle of domestic possessions, leisure activities and wider social horizons. Colchester became a shopping centre, offering these goods and services to its own region. At the same time a growing military presence in the town not only enhanced its urban appeal, but also generated new economic opportunities.

Cloth trade decline

The 1715 weavers' strike had demonstrated their economic importance within the industry. In 1724 they rioted for higher wages and in 1727 the justices confirmed by-laws allowing them to supervise their trade. The following year the Dutch Bay Governors, owing money to the corporation and rent for the Bay Hall, disbanded their company and ceased to regulate the industry. Henceforth, a shrinking body of

baymakers were regulated by market forces. Bankruptcies followed, but as late as 1768 there were still 25 clothiers in the town, reduced to 10 by 1790. These remaining businesses were large, long-established concerns, an effective local oligarchy, a far cry from the bustling 100 baymakers of 1707. New blood did not enter the industry; sons did not follow their fathers. As with clothiers, so with weavers. By 1790 there were still some four hundred in the town, though by now some were weaving in silk.

80 James Kay, who invented the flying shuttle while supervising his father's woollen mills in Colchester.

81   Great swathes of outer Colchester were still wholly rural. Note the woman spinning outside this picturesque cottage.

82   Sir Isaac Rebow, the political ruler of Colchester for half a generation.

Otherwise there were few significant changes to an industry supervised by the capitalist clothiers in the traditional way and fatally dependent on London factors for finding their distant markets. The flying shuttle developed by James Kay, who worked for a while in Colchester, was adopted, as were horse-driven 'roughing machines' to raise the nap on the cloth. Wool-washing machines were installed, though few changes took place in spinning, most of which was still done on spinning wheels in surrounding villages by women and girls: up to ten thousand at the height of the trade. It was 1794 before we find a Colchester clothier employing his own spinning jennies.

The decline of the cloth trade led to a decline in population, at least until the 1740s. There were other negative consequences too. The town's first newspaper, launched in 1733,

83 The castle from the north on its earthworks in 1725, before Charles Grey put domes and turrets on its corners. Behind the castle is All Saints Church. Far right stands the great tower of St Nicholas Church which collapsed when being repaired, destroying much of the church. The tower was eventually replaced in wood. Tenter frames stand below the castle, and Middle Mill, a fulling mill, stands on the river. The Roman wall runs across what is today Castle Park.

collapsed: hereafter Chelmsford provided the main Essex newspaper, Ipswich the main Colchester news. Colchester's grammar school did not flourish; a public water supply, based on a reservoir inside the Balkerne Gate, failed from neglect; houses stood empty or were demolished. Most disastrously, in 1742, the town lost its charter. This arose from the bitterness and corrupt practices that accompanied the arrival of party politics in corporation affairs.

The 'Glorious Revolution' of 1689, which had seen the replacement of James II by William and Mary, had enabled local Whigs to secure political power in Colchester. The dominant figure was Sir Isaac Rebow, who was variously mayor, alderman, recorder, high steward and ten times M.P. for the town. For services thus

rendered, he was knighted by William III at Harwich during one of the King's frequent trips to Holland. Rebow was of Dutch descent and his wealth came from cloth and inheritance, but as a political 'boss' he was ruthless in his pursuit of electoral victory. During bitter party fighting in the 1690s the practice grew of shamelessly 'selling' free burgess status to 'foreigners', who were political supporters, in order to sway election results. Such activity led to disputed elections and legal suits which, with the cost of several new charters, told heavily on the borough's fragile finances. The Dutch Bay Hall, the borough fields, even the Harsnett Library, were mortgaged to raise money. In 1712 the Whig group mortgaged the large Severalls Estate, as Kingswood Heath was now called, for £1,000, twice the borough's annual income. Then in 1722 they leased it (still mortgaged) for 99 years to Daniel Defoe, a prominent Whig as well as a leading literary figure, for a lump sum of £1,000 and £120 per annum. All this debt was serviced by further borrowing.

By 1741 the Tories were in control. Vicious party in-fighting created a situation where none of the current aldermen was deemed properly elected. The Assembly ceased to exist. The loss of civic responsibility was further dramatic evidence of civic decline. With no charter there were no borough courts and no jurisdiction over the river and the fishery, until a 1750 Act of Parliament re-established new channel commissioners. Meanwhile the channel deteriorated, the oyster fishery was plundered, and, with no one to collect them, rates were withheld and householders were reluctant to repair roads. Another casualty was the centralised borough workhouse which had been run quite successfully for the past 45 years. This too ceased, to be replaced by a separate poor-law provision for each of 16 parishes, though no longer subsidised by the 'fines' for poor workmanship which the Bay Hall had supplied.

These unhappy consequences lasted 22 years. With no initial move either by the town's elite or by the borough's M.P.s to secure a new charter, a Charter Club was formed by the freemen: they, after all, had lost their privileges. The key role was taken by William Mayhew, a lawyer, who eventually persuaded two Parliamentary candidates, Charles Gray (Tory) and Isaac Martin Rebow (Whig), to press for a new charter in return for the full support of the freemen and (by implication) an uncontested election. The two compromise M.P.s initiated a period of political stability. Gray is also remembered for 'restoring' Colchester Castle to give it its present appearance, during his long residence in what is now Hollytree Museum.

The restored charter of 1763 was greeted with some celebration, as Colchester began to show some alternative to decades of decline. Across the nation the rise of a consumer society facilitated an industrious if not an industrial revolution. Perhaps 30 per cent of the town's population could now afford 'decencies' as well as bare necessities. Equally significantly, luxuries formerly accessible only to the gentry could, by mass production, become affordable to the middling sort. Towns like Colchester were centres of manufacture, distribution, specialised services and entertainment. As the largest in Essex, serving a wide rural hinterland, Colchester found its feet as a market town. The sheer size and dominance of London meant that no town within a 50-mile radius could be a regional capital. The food needs of the Metropolis were immense, however, and Essex agriculture benefited. Colchester, therefore, could meet the rising needs of the farming community in coals, improved farm buildings, food, and provisions, as well as supply the growing range of personal and domestic goods which their new-found affluence afforded.

This operated at both a wholesale and a retail level. Colchester High Street became full of glass-fronted shops, specialising in fashionable clothing, groceries, furniture, leather goods, books, stationery, glassware and china. Only a wide catchment area sustained such diversity: market day became crucial to the town's economy. Smallpox epidemics were feared (and there were several) because they deterred the country cousins from coming to town, including the farmers' wives who shopped while their husbands assembled for the sale of corn and livestock. Social diversity was reflected in the range of premises, from smart High Street 'emporiums' to mere back street stalls. Butchers and bakers, those basic food merchants, operated at both ends of the market. Substantial premises held extensive stock, requiring, in the days before refrigeration, extensive cellarage. Wine merchants in particular

84 A High Street grocery shop, already 184 years old when this mid-Victorian picture was drawn.

built large and elaborate brick cellars, extending below the main streets. Ice from Norwegian lakes was imported at the Hythe.

Larger grocers in turn supplied and financed village shops within a 20-mile radius, buying goods in bulk not just from London, but from Yorkshire, Lancashire and Cheshire. Rock salt from Liverpool regularly came in at the Hythe, some of it being further refined at salt works on Hythe Quay. Colchester stay-makers would travel to villages, fit ladies in their own homes or hire fitting rooms in inns as far apart as Ipswich, Harwich, Sudbury and Chelmsford.

A Colchester military tailor, contracting to make uniforms for whole regiments, employed 40 tailors himself, and subcontracted weaving to firms as distant as Haverhill and London. After 1780 large warehouses began to appear selling cheap goods, mass-produced in London, to customers further down the social scale. Elsewhere special sales were held of middle-priced china and glass. At every point 'London fashion' was a two-edged marketing sword, either seeking to discredit a local product or to promote it as a cheap but indistinguishable alternative to the truly London equivalent.

85 Photograph taken in 1907 of a tallow candle factory on Barrack Street still operating old equipment and dating from the 1790s.

86 A Colchester-made clock of about 1750 by Barnaby Dammant.

Many of these goods were manufactured locally. As with the cloth trade itself, still the town's largest employer, master craftsmen began to employ a range of outworkers, either in their own homes or in small workshops, sometimes subdividing the stages of manufacture. Shoemakers, tailors and building workers headed the local crafts, but wigmakers, cutlers, printers, bookbinders and saddlers can also be found, plus a rope maker, a gunsmith and a cork-cutter. Candlestick makers and clay pipe makers were not popular neighbours; hat makers risked industrial poisoning. Clocks, and to a lesser extent watches, were assembled in some numbers by Colchester clockmakers who formed family dynasties. Individual parts – wheels, springs and plates – were probably mass-produced in London and assembled in the locality.

As always, inns provided accommodation and refreshment, a congenial venue for conducting business, more formal events being housed

in a large rear room where political clubs might meet or doctors hold surgeries on market day, offering such advanced services as smallpox inoculation. Road transport was constantly on the increase and, since William of Orange had become King, the Essex Great Road from London to Harwich had been maintained to turnpike standard, its frequent and affluent travellers inviting the unwelcome attention of occasional London highwaymen. From Harwich boats sailed for the continent. Thus it was that in August 1763 the great Dr Johnson ate at the *White Hart* in Colchester, its entrance marked today by Bank Passage, before seeing his biographer Boswell off on the Harwich packet.

The same London road brought much agricultural traffic through the town, heading for London. Drovers from as far away as Scotland stopped at the *Rose & Crown* in East Street with their herds, prior to fattening them on Essex pasture. Next to the Moot Hall in

87 Colchester High Street in 1858 with hurdles erected for the Saturday livestock market. Left stands the *Cups Inn*, beyond that the 1844 town hall, with St Runwald's Church (see p.25), restored in 1760, just visible behind two blurred figures.

88 Middle Mill, one of Colchester six watermills, once used for fulling cloth, photographed about 1860. The large chimney belongs to the steam engine at the silk mill (see page 84).

89 A view of the Hythe from Clingo Hill in 1741. Note the hoys sailing in on high tide, the houses on Hythe Quay, the imported cut timber, the site of Hythe Bridge and the town of Colchester beyond. Three windmills stand near Mill Street, one on Butt Road. All the churches can be identified, including St Leonard's on Hythe Hill.

High Street the *Cups Inn* played host to VIPs such as the future King of France, Admiral Lord Nelson and the Duke of Wellington. From 1754 the London mail arrived daily at the *Kings Head* in Head Street. By 1762 a daily coach went to and from London, with a wagon service weekly. These, and the improving transport of farmers and gentry, gave coach builders, blacksmiths, wheelwrights, grooms and hay dealers increasing business. In all, the town now housed 80 inns, the largest of which kept horses and vehicles for hire. By 1800 the *King's Head* boasted 30 beds for travellers, stabling for 100 horses, 14 acres of pasture, coach houses, hay barns and a granary holding 500 quarters of corn. They also served fresh venison every Tuesday.

An agricultural hinterland sustained much agricultural processing. Millers were numerous, not just because of the town's many watermills, several of which still did fulling, but also because of the town's rural parishes in the Liberties. Brewing was an industry being increasingly industrialised. Though some inns still brewed their own ales and small beer was produced on farms and in manor houses, commercial breweries emerged, often owning their own maltings or a string of local inns. North Hill and East Hill, both standing conveniently on a spring line, provided popular sites. The town boasted three distilleries, a soapworks and two large tanneries. Quite large maltings were developed at the Hythe, their product going to Holland or to the great porter breweries in

London. Here Ben Truman commissioned his pale malt from John Kemp, the finest producer in Essex. Though farming at Sible Hedingham, Kemp made his malt at the Hythe.

Despite the problems it faced with its long tidal channel, the Hythe was an active port and held its own throughout the century, increasing its tonnage and still able, at high water, to accommodate the coastal sailing ships, the hoys. Timber and iron came from Sweden, building tiles and brandy from Rotterdam, fuller's earth from Kent and ever more coal from Tyneside. Large quantities of wheat and significant amounts of malt and barley went to London, whence came raw wool for the clothiers and a range of 'general goods'. Wheat shipments rose from around 10,000 quarters in 1700 to 80,000 by 1810; coal imports from 4,500 tons in 1725 to 23,000 after 1800.

Gradually Hythe Quay became home to an assortment of industrial activities, rising from 10 establishments in 1761 to 41 by 1810. As well as the maltings and salt works, there were nine coalyards, eight granaries, a brick kiln, coke ovens, a lime kiln and a foundry. It was a significant industrial centre. Merchants, themselves resident on the quay, might use their skills to multiple effect. One shipbuilder dealt in corn, timber and coal, owned half a ship and the *Rising Sun* pub and cultivated four acres. Shipbuilding remained a Hythe activity throughout the century, up to ten boats being built per year, mostly of 10 to 25 tons burthen. In 1800 the port had 145 registered vessels employing 434 men.

For much of this period smuggling was an extensive coastal activity, tolerated by a large section of rural society. We do not know how much local tradesmen dealt in contraband goods or how far Colchester's economy benefited from the illegal trade. The custom house still standing on Hythe Quay had warehouses where seized contraband was kept, which, subsequently sold, was usually valued at £800 to £1,000 a year,

90 The former Customs House on Hythe Quay has a Georgian front from about 1720.

though once at £2,350. In 1748 smugglers raiding the custom house made off with, *inter alia*, 15 hundredweight of impounded tea. Such a haul provides a brief view of the submerged half of the illicit iceberg.

Tea, indeed, was the symbol of the new gentility. The English tea ceremony, with sets of matching china, tea pots, elegant tables, table cloths and polite conversation epitomised that emulation of social superiors which characterised this age, as a former luxury became available to all but the poorest classes. Typical is the 1766 newspaper advertisement announcing:

John Mills, tea dealer from Mssrs Twining in London, proposes to open next week a tea warehouse ... in High Street Colchester where those who favour him with their custom may depend on being served with tea, coffee and chocolate as good and upon as reasonable terms as in London.

Tea smuggling was a response to high taxation. To sell tea legally therefore required a government licence, costing 5s. 6d. According to official records in 1784 there were 179 licensed tea dealers in Colchester (compared with 100 at Ipswich). Even though this figure probably applies to the Colchester *district*, it demonstrates how far a nation of shopkeepers had become a nation of tea-drinkers. It also shows that trade directories totally omit an underclass of retailers, often women trading from their own parlour to their immediate neighbourhood, with a set of scales and the capacity to offer generous credit or 'tick'.

The mention of credit underlines an important Colchester reality. A large percentage of its population was self-employed. Citizens encountered one another less as employers and workers than as buyers and sellers. Craftsmen could rent accommodation cheaply or work from their own home, often setting up in business after years as journeymen. The larger the operation, the more start-up capital was

91 Colchester's two banks issued their own notes. This came from 'Round's Bank' (now Barclays in High Street).

needed. Houses were mortgaged, wider family resources were drawn on, fellow workers formed partnerships. It was, therefore, an important moment when John Mills the tea dealer also opened the Colchester & Essex Bank at 3, High Street in 1787 in partnership with the Twining brothers. In this he was institutionalising what had happened for centuries: the loaning of money by large traders. In Colchester the wine merchant Charles Whaley had lent money since the 1730s, establishing a bank (today Barclays in High Street) with the Crickitts in 1774. In 1790 George Round became the dominant partner, while Mills and his son were joined by John Bawtree. Round's Bank and Bawtree's Bank, as they became popularly known, were to serve Colchester's business community for most of the 19th century.

The new genteel lifestyle also boosted Colchester as a centre of entertainment. Both the *White Hart* and the *King's Head* held monthly assemblies and balls in their large assembly rooms. In 1764 the Norwich Company built a theatre to the rear of the moot hall where plays by Shakespeare and Sheridan were performed. Concerts were held in local inns and an orchestral rendering of Handel's 'Messiah' in 1763 involved London artists and the boys of St Paul's choir. Such performances might be timed to coincide with the opening of the St Dennis Fair, still a major Colchester event, where the Public Breakfast for 200 was all about being seen, rather than being fed.

This underlines how much leisure activity hinged on social patronage. Colchester now had something of a resident gentry: families with wealth and connection rather than large businesses. A few had moved in from London, appreciating Colchester's daily contact with 'town'; others represented the accumulation of baymaking money by marriage and inheritance. Some quite lavish houses and gardens were laid out, notably at the top of East Hill (demolishing rows of cottages in

92 Social life in Colchester is caught in this drawing by Dunthorne of 'The Tea Room at a Colchester Ball', apparently held at the *White Hart Inn.*

the process), and surviving Georgian town houses can be seen at points nearby. Members of the professional classes: clergy, physicians, lawyers, estate agents, held equivalent status, augmented by a growing band of rural gentry and upwardly mobile farmers. Below them were a rising number of small business owners and white-collar occupations. Together the middle ranks of society formed perhaps 20 per cent of the population.

We should not, however, overstate Colchester's cultural standing. The leading promoter of Colchester assemblies, Joseph Gibbs, was from Ipswich and ran almost as many assemblies at Dedham, while the elegance of Bury St Edmunds at this date (and the size of its assembly rooms) far outshone that of Colchester. The same is true of intellectual endeavour. Newspapers kept those who cared aware of national events, yet Colchester could not sustain its own newspaper. Individuals like the Rev. Philip Morant, rector of St Mary's and author of a 1748 *History of Colchester*, kept large libraries, and Charles Gray, a Trustee of the British Museum and for long the town's M.P., even formed a Castle Book Club (a library in fact), but by 1790 it had only 30 members, 10 of whom were clergy.

More popular entertainment was provided by horse races held on Mile End Heath, by cricket matches played for half-guinea hats, by Mr Green's pioneer ballooning demonstrations and by the formation in 1798 of the East Essex Foxhounds. Misconduct in inns continued to exercise the magistrates, as it had always done, where cockfighting or performing bears continued in defiance of the rulings of the borough court. Such savage amusement equally offended the godly. Though 18th-century Colchester, like the nation, had its share of clergy more notable for their learning than their ardour, and a Nonconformist community whose members were 'men of habit more than men of piety', we must recognise the fundamental importance of religion in the town. Parishes, in addition to their responsibility for the poor law, provided the basis for a good deal of community action. This was particularly true as the Evangelical Revival made its mark on Colchester.

As early as 1758 John Wesley preached to the small congregation of proto-Methodists in the town on St John's Green at the St Dennis Fair, and visited them almost annually for the next 32 years. From 1781 Robert Storry was an active Evangelical at the town church of

93 Lion Walk Church, known as 'the round church', was actually octagonal. Built in 1766 with an 1816 extension, it replaced an even earlier building.

St Peter's, attracting to Colchester the newly ordained Patrick Brontë (future father of the Brontë sisters), and encouraging the important Simeon Trust at Cambridge to secure the living of the church. Storry was in consequence followed by the influential Rev. William Marsh. During his stay from 1814 to 1829 some 22 male members of his congregation became missionaries or clergymen, and such was his legendary status that when in 1852 he returned to preach at St Peter's over two thousand people came to hear him.

From 1788 Sunday schools were established in the town and over the next 20 years new organisations promoted earnest Christianity. Anglicans supported missionaries; Quakers were active in the anti-slavery campaign. Religious energy established the Colchester & Essex

Hospital on Lexden Road and fuelled the drive to advance education. In 1812 a National (i.e. Church of England) central school was formed, combining the Bluecoat School with non-denominational Sunday schools. This was an issue which concerned Nonconformity too, and the parallel establishment of a central British (i.e. Nonconformist) school and Nonconformist Sunday schools ensured sectarian competition over education during the Victorian period. Elsewhere schools for 'young gentlemen' and 'young ladies' provided for the middle classes.

Nonconformists now formed perhaps a quarter of Colchester's population and were becoming a dynamic minority, at once evangelical and high-minded. Devoutness went hand in hand with rational enquiry. Isaac Taylor, minister of the St Helen's Lane Chapel and father of the children's writers Jane and Ann Taylor, held lectures in his own house for fifty to seventy young men on technical and scientific subjects. His daughters' immensely popular books of hymns and poems, of which 'Twinkle, Twinkle Little Star' is the most famous, anticipated the new moral earnestness which forged the Victorian Age. The Colchester Philosophical Society, founded in 1820 and a more 'establishment' body, accumulated its own museum and debated such topics as heat, electricity and 'the variety of human species' at its monthly meetings.

The French Wars

The regular outbreaks of war which puncuated the 18th century did not merely disrupt Colchester's shrinking cloth trade: they also brought soldiers to the town. From 1741 Lexden Heath was cleared of undergrowth and used for large encampments during the summer months: up to ten thousand troops might be involved. Royal reviews, 'sham battles' and cavalry manoeuvres provided a spectator sport. More significant were the business opportunities for supplying bread, fodder or fuel. Within Colchester the military were viewed as a mixed blessing. Billeting in inns and public houses under powers granted to the government under the Mutiny Act were a strain on law and order, if the source of some trade. So were the regular forays of recruiting sergeants. In 1778 the *Ipswich Journal* noted that the principal inns in Colchester had 150 men each – a considerable disruption of normal business. For this they were paid 4d. per soldier per day, a rate not increased since 1690. Petitions regularly went to the War Office, notably on the outbreak of war against Republican France in 1793, requesting the establishment of barracks in the town.

This time the government responded, mindful of the sheer numbers involved and the imminent threat of invasion. A vast hutted

94 A surviving uniform of the Colchester Loyal Volunteers was sufficiently small to fit this youthful model.

encampment for infantry was built on greenfield land to the south of Magdalen Street. By 1805 it housed 6,600 (sleeping two to a bed): the largest garrison in Britain. Artillery and cavalry barracks were also built, the former housing 1,000 men at its height. In addition there were brick-built houses for officers and a hospital able to hold 500 casualties: a phenomenal number for that date. Part of this building was re-erected on Lexden Road in 1820 to form the Colchester & Essex Hospital. Though many of the larger contracts for building and supplying this garrison went to London, it still impacted greatly on the Colchester district, from 'hucksters and Jews' trading at the barrack gates, to William Hawkins who brought timber in huge quantities to the Hythe, and John Bawtree who built the massive St Botolph's Brewery, which was powered by Colchester's first steam engine, a Boulton & Watt. Colchester's controversial but powerful town clerk, Frank Smythies, invested heavily in

95 Colchester's medieval North Gate, at the bottom of North Hill, painted by Edward Eyre in about 1780, after its rather crude widening in 1774. The steelyard on the right served to weigh wagons leaving town in compliance with legislation proscribing wheel width and wagon weights.

inns. Soldiers, many of whom were militiamen, were allowed to earn money helping with the harvest. Soldier-civilian marriages were solemnised in local churches. Camp followers were a problem. Naked soldiers bathing in the river upset Sunday walkers.

From the commanding general downwards, officers greatly enlivened the social scene. A new assembly room was built in the *Cups Hotel* and a large new theatre in Queen Street. Picnic parties on the beach at Walton-on-the-Naze were the prelude to its development as a seaside resort in the 1820s by a group of Colchester businessmen.

The long wars were also marked by unprecedented levels of inflation and great consequent hardship. John Wesley wrote of the poverty of his converts. Eld Lane Baptist Church

noted 'many [are] nearly starving for want of employ ... the times are awful beyond expression.' Grain was seized by crowds in 1782 and 1789 and in 1795, a bad year, a collection of £700 financed 4,000 food tickets for the poor.

Yet the defeat of Napoleon and the end of war in 1815 dealt Colchester a double blow. Farmers who had enjoyed unprecedented profits while the war restricted food imports faced a big fall in the price they received for grain and, to a lesser extent, for livestock. Colchester, the farmers' market, suffered too. One prominent High Street draper claimed his trade had fallen by one-third. Simultaneously, the wartime garrison was run down and then dismantled. Its extensive wooden huts, forges, stables, thousands of used bricks, 40 wheelbarrows and 600 horses were sold in a

96 This 1878 photo taken from the top of a rebuilt St Nicholas Church spire (see page 117) shows how densely packed were the red-roofed houses of central Colchester. Note the ruts left by wheeled traffic.

series of large auctions. Sheds in the Tendring Hundred still betrayed their origins five decades later. Colchester became strangely quiet and lacking in custom.

Despite such hardship it remained a fairly orderly town, spared the unholy squalor and simmering social tensions of Britain's new industrial cities. Colchester's modest physical growth, its large middle class, its paternalistic, pre-industrial trades all contributed to this. Green fields lay all around, gardens abounded within the ancient walls and both visitors and residents considered it a healthy town, famous for growing auriculas. American independence

97 Colchester's massive silk throwing mill, brick-built and driven by steam, was opened by Stephen Brown in 1826, an unusual addition to a market town.

Though expanding in population, Colchester continued to slide down the league table of British towns. In 1801 it was 33rd; in 1841 about 70th. The cloth trade was now dead and the silk industry, migrating out of London, had scarcely taken root in the town. The main exception was a large modern silk-throwing factory run by Stephen Brown whose background was in corn milling. The raw silk came from Italy and the mill, by the river, employed up to four hundred women, some as young as ten. This apart, Colchester remained a market town of shops and inns, traditional crafts, agriculture, horticulture and related industries like brewing, milling and malting.

Its markets, however, were growing, as the surrounding rural population rose by 60 per cent between 1760 and 1800, and a further 45 per cent by 1830. In-migration to Colchester was marked, as young people sought employment: men as labourers, women as servants. Physically the town expanded inwards: more properties were built on garden ground; new terraces appeared within the existing urban envelope. In 1811 Colchester's Channel Commissioners were reconstituted, taking on additional responsibility for 'improvement' to the town's infrastructure. Run by an oligarchy of interested businessmen, the new commissioners remained strictly non-political and over the next 60 years proved more able than the town council to advance the necessary process of cleaning, sewering and lighting the town. Colchester now had its own newspaper, the *Colchester Express*, its streets were gas-lit and a history published in 1825 proclaimed: 'perhaps no town in England in proportion to its size and population supports so many benevolent and charitable institutions as Colchester', 20 of which are then described. Colchester was well qualified to enter the Victorian Age.

and the French Revolution had spawned a host of radical ideas. We know that Colchester tailors avidly read William Cobbett's *Political Register* and that Richard Patmore, one of the last baymakers, was prosecuted for distributing Tom Paine's *Rights of Man*, but when rural north Essex exploded into violence in 1830-1 over the introduction of threshing machines in the so-called 'Swing riots', there were few echoes in Colchester. Rather the town threw its energies (for and against) into the political campaign of the Radical Daniel Whittle Harvey for the reform of Parliament.

Eight
Pride and Progress
1830-1914

In 1830 Colchester had bad government and bad drains. Three Acts of Parliament, fundamental for the future of urban Britain, addressed this. They also launched Westminster government's increasing control of local affairs over the next 150 years.

In 1832 came the landmark Great Reform Act, more significant for the defeat it inflicted on the old order than for the number of new voters it created. Colchester already had a large electorate to choose its two M.P.s made up of those who qualified as freemen by apprenticeship as well as the hereditary freemen, their sons and their grandsons, irrespective of where they lived. Consequently general elections, famous for riot and revelry, also became family reunions. Thoughtful candidates would pay the single fare for non-resident freemen to travel to Colchester. The return fare came after they had voted – in public. So many qualified freemen now lived in London that in 1831 one candidate chartered a boat to bring them by sea to the Hythe.

The Reform Act enfranchised resident freemen only plus male owners of a house with a high rateable value. These 'new' voters tended to be middle-class and middle-aged, with a distinct preference for a quiet life and the success of agriculture, the town's main economic support. One paradoxical result of the Great Reform Act, a Radical triumph, was to render the Colchester constituency a safe place for Tory M.P.s for a generation to come.

In 1834 the Whig government lost what Radical support they still had when they introduced the 'new' poor law. This required the systematic building of new workhouses to which the poor must go, if unable to support themselves. There was to be no more 'outdoor relief'(payments in cash or kind to the resident poor) funded by household rates, such as Colchester had pioneered as long ago as 1557. In practice Colchester, as elsewhere, continued some outdoor relief, if only because it was less expensive. But the threat of incarceration in Colchester's new workhouse hung like a cloud over the destitute for almost a century. Particularly, it was the fear of the elderly that they would end their days in 'the house' or

98 Colchester High Street from the east in 1834, showing assorted countryfolk in front of a half-ruined St Nicholas Church with its makeshift wooden tower. St Runwald's and the Obelisk in the distance sustain the feel of an old market town. Only the *George Hotel* (far right) is there today.

99 High Street from the west in 1862: a very early 'instant' photograph of the Saturday livestock market showing the Fire Office, a line of cabs, farmers examining a stack cloth, and blurred sheep entering the sheep-pens.

In 1835 the Whig government introduced a universal reform of borough government. To provide themselves with background (and incriminating) evidence, commissioners were sent to suspect boroughs, one of which was Colchester. At this date the three-tier borough assembly (i.e. town council) was almost totally Tory and Anglican and viewed the arrival of a Whig commissioner as a declaration of war. Documents requested by the commissioner, Mr Hogg, were not supplied (they appear to have been lost) and the town clerk adopted a policy of outright non-cooperation, the bitterness of which is aptly summed up in the letter he wrote to the newspaper at the enquiry's end:

> The commissioner is now reaching Mrs Hog and the little hogs, having vermin-like been crawling over the country to fatten and gorge on filth wherever he can find it and make it up where there was none.

'the spike' as it was later called. The new workhouse (later St Mary's Hospital), was a substantial complex of buildings. It seems to have been run properly, even humanely, throughout its long history, but the dramatic fall in the cost of the new poor law (and consequent fall in the rates) explains why the most desperate in Victorian Colchester were also the most silent.

Amid such statesmanship, Colchester's ancient corporation, first established in 1372, sank into history, to be replaced by a modern town council of 24: three-quarters elected by all ratepayers for a three-year period; one quarter to be aldermen, selected by the council itself and serving for six years. From the outset,

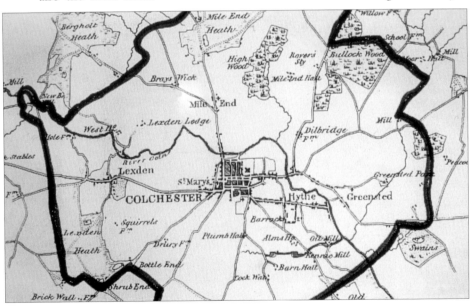

100 This plan of the Colchester Parliamentary constituency of 1832 shows how little the town had expanded since 1610 (see page 53) with Mile End, Greenstead, Monkwick, Shrub End and Lexden still wholly rural.

bitter partisan politics dulled their effective-
ness. Both parties, when they had a majority
of councillors, were prepared to fill the aldermanic bench with defeated councillors of their
own persuasion.

The handful of officers were also party
appointments, starting with the town clerk,
always a local solicitor with an existing local
practice, and widely viewed as the *leader* of
the party in power. Initially the Whigs (soon
to call themselves Liberals) won power and
seized the spoils of office. Within two years
the Tories (soon to be Conservatives) regained
their majority, replaced most of the officers, and
stayed in power for 42 years, during which time
there was not a single Liberal mayor.

Many able Nonconformists consequently
refused to run for office and it was fortunate
that Colchester's fragile infrastructure was
in the care of the non-political Channel
Commissioners. Much of their effort went
into the slow process (slow because of their
limited resources) of lighting, cleansing and
sewering the town. As its population grew,
Colchester, like most of urban Britain, faced a
public health problem. Since that most dramatic
killer, cholera, had a minimal impact in 1833-4
and made no subsequent visitation, few of the
'great' and not all of the 'good' felt a sense of
urgency. The Liberal chairman of the Channel
Commissioners, John Bawtree Harvey, led the
campaign for half a lifetime.

Ignorance was another enemy. A survey
conducted by Harvey in 1858 showed that
many in Colchester took their water from some
450 private wells, many of which were a short
distance from a cess pit. The owners could not
all be blamed, since the waterworks company,
a profit-making venture, did not consider it
economic to extend their pipes to two-thirds
of the town's population. When an 'Inspector
of Nuisances' was appointed, he requested a
man in Magdalen Street to remove a large
dung heap he had accumulated over many

101 The late Victorian Hythe was dominated
by brick warehouses, Thames barges and lighters
bringing up coal from Wivenhoe.

years from neighbouring privies. Seeing the
pile gone, the inspector knocked on the door
to thank the man, only to find that he had
moved the heap into his kitchen. After all, it
was his stock in trade, for sale to local market
gardeners. Such an anecdote would probably
have disturbed a town council of 1360; now
it was 1860.

Financial parsimony also limited the
commissioners' efforts to extend gas lighting
throughout the borough, and it almost
torpedoed Harvey's plan to install quite
minimal sewers under the main streets. This
was in part because the commissioners were
more exercised by their historic responsibility
for the river and the port. In 1842 Ipswich
finally opened its new wet dock, a 24-hour
port which was to play a major part in that
town's rapid economic growth over the next 75
years. The Great Eastern Railway would soon
charge more to transport goods from London
to Chelmsford than from London to Ipswich,
simply because that town could play the
railway off against the river. Chelmsford had
no such realistic alternative. Did Colchester?
Twice in the 1840s owners of wharves at the

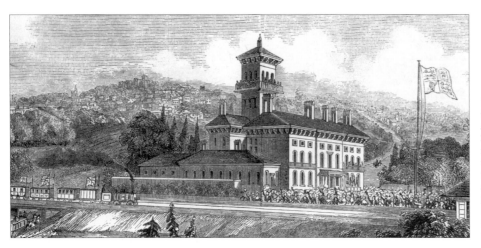

102 Artist's view of the first train arriving at Colchester North Station from Ipswich in 1846. Beyond the *Victoria Hotel* the artist has built a Tuscan hilltown, greatly exaggerating Colchester's size and distance from the railway.

Hythe sought in vain to persuade Colchester to build an ambitious ship canal from the Hythe to Wivenhoe. Partly the town lacked the entrepreneurial will to attempt it, but mainly the tidal channel did not merit it.

Nevertheless, the Hythe did remain an active, though declining, port and the commissioners raised (via dues) and spent (by dredging) a good deal of money keeping it so. In return, Colchester did keep the railway competitive, particularly in coal. Thomas Moy built up the largest coal delivery business in Eastern England using its rail network, but his ability to bring coal by sea to the Hythe, was crucial to his success. The Hythe also benefited by the evolution of the Thames sailing barge, a triumph of timber technology, able to sail in shallow waters and to marshal coastal winds. Other significant Hythe cargoes were grain and malt going out; timber, general goods and Kentish ragstone coming in. Ipswich, however, was able to win the majority of the inland trade of South Suffolk; Maldon supplied most of the materials for the railway advancing towards Colchester.

The Railway
The railway arrived in 1843: two miles away from the Hythe at the greenfield site where North Station now stands. Owners of land behind Lexden Road wanted such high prices that the Eastern Counties Railway came in on the opposite side of the river valley. Members of Colchester's business community thought it the town's biggest blunder. Goods arriving for High Street had to negotiate the steep slope of North Hill and the questionable stability of North Bridge, which was rapidly rebuilt in iron. The problem was to an extent eased when two further railway terminals were built: one at St Botolph's Corner (now Colchester Town); one, crucially, at the Hythe with (eventually) a railway line along the quay.

At North Station the railway halted, the company having exhausted the capital which was supposed to finance a line to Norwich. This was particularly galling to Ipswich businessmen who had invested in the line. Their response was to build their own railway south to Colchester and north to Norwich. By now the Eastern Counties Railway had secured an alternative route to Norwich via Cambridge and the Colchester terminal found itself the centre of a 'railway war'. Connections with Ipswich trains were deliberately kept so bad as to prompt jokes in the London press. Thus: 'yesterday an 18-year-old man, caught at Ipswich travelling on a juvenile ticket, said in his defence, "I was 13 when we left London!" '

103 Artist's impression of the new livestock market opened at Middleborough to effect easier links with the railway.

Indeed, the public works of Colchester had a bad press for most of the mid-Victorian period.

North Bridge was rumoured several inches too short and a new Hythe Bridge collapsed when half-built. But there *were* attempts at progress. A new Corn Exchange in High Street reflected a rising agricultural prosperity, crucial to the town's immediate well-being. A new town hall opened in 1844 was less successful. Unable to afford the lowest tender, the council gave the contract to a local syndicate whose structure was jerry-built and standing on a sewer. They also demolished Colchester's ancient Moot Hall, a multi-period building dating back to Norman times.

The railway, for all its inauspicious start, was the most important change to Colchester in the century. Initially, of course, the world of stagecoaches – inns, horses, coach-building, turnpikes – suffered. But High Street inns soon collected customers direct from the station, forcing the new *Victoria Hotel* there to close. A community of railway workers grew up along an extended North Station Road and by 1900 the railway supplied at least 400 Colchester jobs,

not to mention the sons of railwaymen sent down the line to jobs elsewhere. The town's expanding Saturday livestock market, held for centuries in High Street, was relocated a short distance from North Station at Middleborough. Here London dealers could buy live meat and transport it by rail to Smithfield Market for slaughter and sale the following Monday. In due course the Colchester market became the largest in the Eastern Counties.

Closeness to London enabled the leather merchant F.W. Warmington to foster a shoemaking trade tied to London's widening suburban markets. Hyam Hyam, the son of a German Jewish immigrant, nurtured in Colchester new techniques for making ready-made men's clothing, based on small workshops supervised by one tailor, the bulk of the sewing being done by young women. The railway enabled his sons to become the largest providers in Britain. Cloth cut in bulk in London was sent down by rail and made up by women, not only in Colchester homes and workshops but in villages up to ten miles away, much as spinning for the cloth trade had been done 100 years before. The development of the

104 Specialist craft workshops, such as William Bruce's coachworks near the bottom of Hythe Hill, were far more characteristic of Victorian Colchester than were large factories.

sewing machine not only meant spectacular productivity gains, but the establishment of Colchester factories where some of the first industrial sewing machines in Britain were installed.

Gradually Colchester's shopkeepers took advantage of the railway's supply of mass-produced goods on a national, indeed international, scale. Coal and grain merchants benefited from a widening network of branch lines, to Wivenhoe, Brightlingsea, Walton and Halstead. The army of local craftsmen faced serious competition where their goods were made by hand in penny numbers, even though the number of local customers was now growing.

A few specialist entrepreneurs found themselves world markets. Ben Cant, from a family of market gardeners, came to specialise

in roses, winning so many prizes and cups at national competitions as to claim to be the best in Britain. Via railway and steamship he built up a client base which covered not only the U.K., but the rest of the world. Orders to 'Cant's of Colchester' could be made from any railway station in Britain. When a nephew, Frank Cant, set up in competition, so many letters arrived addressed simply to 'Cant's of Colchester' that a special postcard was produced by the Post Office asking the sender which 'Cant' they meant. Between them the two rose growers offered almost a thousand varieties.

Lent Watts, son of a bricklayer, took over a small stonemason firm in 1866. Not content with meeting the needs of Colchester's bereaved, he installed steam-driven stone cutting equipment to produce gravestones in bulk, selling via catalogues to customers in Essex,

105 Lent Watts' Castle Steam Stone Works not only placed new industry near the genteel top of East Hill, but demonstrated what might be achieved in market penetration by a provincial firm.

Suffolk and London. He acquired his own quarry at Carrara in Italy where local villagers spent winter evenings carving scallop shells and decorative pieces to appear on marble fireplaces which were sold on a similar mass scale. Watts's son made a long trip to Australia and New Zealand where new bulk supplies of stone were secured and new markets opened up.

The greatest railway-related bonus came when the government decided to re-establish Colchester's garrison at the end of the Crimean War. Initially 2,000 men of the German Legion were accommodated in tents, pending demobilisation. Many married local girls before accepting a government offer to settle in South Africa. Wooden huts, built for use in the Crimea, then housed an infantry garrison of 3,000 between Military and Mersea Roads. From 1862 cavalry barracks for 2,500 men and their horses were built on Butt Road, followed by artillery barracks built in the 1870s. At the end of the century yet more land was acquired, extensive firing ranges were opened at Middlewick and a military hospital and further barracks were built. As headquarters of Eastern Command, Colchester became one of the largest peacetime establishments in the country. One early calculation suggested an additional £60,000 a year was spent in the town. It was undoubtedly more.

The garrison provided business for coal, provisions and fodder merchants, for brewers, tailors and builders. Several hundred yards of cast iron railing were made in a local foundry. Inns in particular flourished, several garrison pubs carrying military names. Initially, law and order was a problem. The 'Battle of St Botolph's Corner' which raged over Christmas 1869 was a belt fight between rival regiments. The civilian police wisely let the military impose its own discipline, which included frog marching drunks (held by wrists and ankles face down) to the barracks, until a soldier suffocated on his own vomit, prompting its abolition. Prostitution became a serious problem leading to the establishment of a local VD hospital. A large officer class left its mark on the social ambience of the town, many living in the expanding middle-class suburb to the south of Lexden Road.

The railway impacted on every aspect of Colchester. Britain was shrinking. As late as 1874 a press notice announced that the clock on the town's new Post Office (built from the increasing number of letters and telegrams) would show 'railway time' rather than local time, Colchester still having public clocks five minutes earlier than London and nine minutes earlier than Oxford. *The Times* newspaper now arrived daily and bank holiday trips to

106 Colchester's new garrison was initially housed in these wooden huts, originally built for use in the Crimea.

Clacton or Walton, themselves products of the new mobility, became accessible to almost all. Even poor children might enjoy the annual Sunday School excursion. Some of the town's businessmen regularly commuted to London. In 1912 several firms combined for a works' outing to distant Blackpool, but what was to transform Colchester was the capacity of railways and steamships to reach every corner of the world – on time.

Late Victorian boom

By 1875 Colchester had made progress, as the Victorians understood the term. But in the eyes of its critics that progress had been modest: Ipswich, for example, was growing far faster. After 1880 the picture changed. The town began to acquire quite a large manu-facturing base. Brewing and milling became more mechanised, but employment oppor-tunities were greatest in 'tailoring', footwear manufacture and engineering.

The ready-made men's clothing industry continued to grow until at least 1910, producing not just for civilian needs but for Empire markets, for institutions like railway companies and asylums, and for the military. Some 1,500 jobs were found in factories, mostly for women, though men did the cutting and much of the

heavier work such as pressing. Most of these factories were owned by London or nationally based firms who were tapping the local pool of skilled, but very cheap, labour. Beyond this, over 3,000 women in Colchester and district worked part-time from their own homes, work being delivered weekly by cart (and later van), their combined incomes sometimes exceeding the meagre returns of male agricultural labour.

Boot and shoe making in Colchester was transformed by the building of factories equipped with American machinery, operated not by skilled craftsmen but by teenage boys and girls. This led to trade union disputes in the town in 1892 and 1895, particularly at the largest such factory, run by the colourful John Kavanagh, who had risen via second-hand clothes dealing to gain the contract for supplying boots to the British Army. In 1898 Kavanagh closed his factory which, purchased by Hollington's of London, soon became Colchester's largest tailoring premises. Severe competition from Northampton and imports from America saw the footwear industry virtually disappear by 1911, having employed almost a thousand people at its height.

By far the most significant new industry was engineering. This grew out of the local foundries where pig iron, imported from the

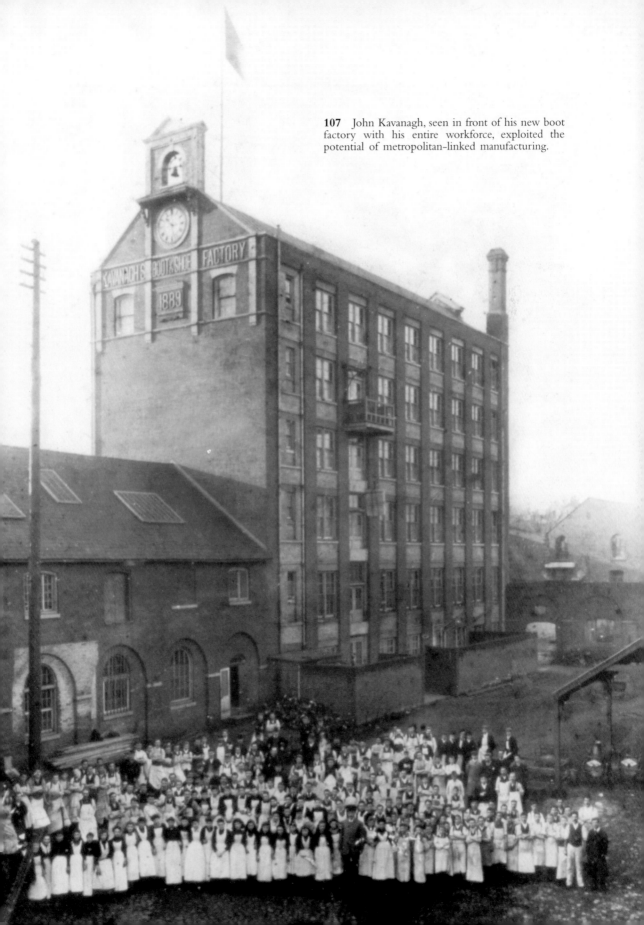

107 John Kavanagh, seen in front of his new boot factory with his entire workforce, exploited the potential of metropolitan-linked manufacturing.

108   Inside Mumford's main erecting shop in Culver Street marine watertube boilers are being assembled, showing that Colchester's engineering factories were both labour- and capital-intensive.

blast furnaces of the north, was melted and moulded into cast-iron products: some for agricultural use; some domestic; some structural such as chaff cutters, fire grates, and lamp posts. More complex agricultural machinery, the work of outside producers like Ransome's of Ipswich, reached Colchester via ironmongers' shops.

It was therefore an important moment when in 1865 James Paxman, for long foreman of Colchester's largest foundry, set up on his own to manufacture agricultural equipment, steam engines and boilers. From an early date, by exhibiting at national shows, he aimed to reach national and international markets. By 1880 with a workforce of 200 he was succeeding. His involvement from 1882 in designing quality engines for electric light generation transformed his business. His appointment to light public exhibitions at South Kensington and Paris, and later to supply power across the British Empire, gave him a worldwide business and great personal wealth. By 1900

he had a workforce of just under a thousand men and a large engineering works on Hythe Hill, covering 12 acres, where gas engines, boilers, mining equipment, compressors and refrigeration equipment were also made.

Just as specialised was Mumford's Culver Street Works which made pumps, marine engines and boilers, and worked closely with Forrestt's the shipbuilders and their successors, Rennie's, at Wivenhoe. The Britannia Engineering Works, beside St Botolph's Station, made a wide range of machine tools, oil engines and (briefly) early motor cars. After 1900 Wood's of Colchester began making electrical fans and the Colchester Lathe Company lathes. All these firms and their principals co-operated closely, buying and promoting one another's goods, never competing. There were other smaller businesses. By 1914, despite serious trade union conflict and recent low levels of profitability, engineering employed almost two thousand men.

109 Jobs at the Great Eastern Railway laundry beside North Station were much sought after. In this posed photograph women use gas irons to press tablecloths and aprons for the Continental train service.

It needs to be recognised, however, that Colchester's late industrial revolution depended, as with the tailoring, on cheap and generally docile labour, in a town where the cost of living was lower than in London and Northern industrial centres. In fact Colchester's *per capita* income was among the lowest of historic parliamentary boroughs. Cheap labour also led London firms like Spottiswoode the printers and Owen Parry's oil mills to relocate to an enlarged Hythe.

Colchester's industrialisation was particularly welcome as Essex agriculture went into a long decline, unable to compete with cheap food imports, despite the desperately low wages of its workforce. Population in the surrounding villages fell. And it was villages to the south of Colchester who most felt the impact of a major earthquake shortly after 9 a.m. on 22 April 1884. It caused a great sensation, tumbled hundreds of chimneys, took down the spire of Lion Walk Church, profited local photographers and

promoted a small influx of tourists. In the long term its impact was insignificant as the drain of people from the land continued.

Many came to Colchester. Men were employed as labourers, women as domestic servants, living over the shop or in the households of Colchester's large and expanding middle class: 2,128 women and 448 men were in domestic work and laundries by 1911. Nor did the town's primary role as a shopping centre falter, as more money fructified in more pockets. The Colchester Co-op alone employed over two hundred staff. The 1911 census records at least 1,300 men and 500 women employed in its 235 shops and its 181 inns and beer shops: one pub for every 208 souls.

The years 1880–1914 were therefore ones of rapid population growth, a prolonged housing boom, the building of factories, impressive public works and spiralling rateable values. While population more than doubled between 1837 and 1897 the value of the penny rate

110 The Oyster Feast of 1902, a vast gathering of the male elite of the town. Mayor Wilson Marriage and his 500 guests depend on gas jets for light when it gets dark.

increased by seven and a half times: and this in an era of overall deflation. This funded a revolution in municipal affairs, accelerated in 1892 by the merging of the commissioners and the town council. A transformed council progressively acquired responsibility for a public library, a museum, a fire brigade, two public parks, a school of science and art, a university extension college, the old grammar school, eight new purpose-built council schools, an electricity supply, a tramway system, the public water supply and sewage system, the port and river navigation, a flourishing and remunerative oyster fishery, the upkeep of 80 miles of road,

by-laws governing all new building and an expanding police force. In the process, of course, the borough had become a major employer. The pursuit of what is termed municipal socialism thus had more than its share of municipal capitalism. There has been nothing like it in Colchester's history before or since. As late as 1871 the borough council had met only quarterly and had but two active committees. By 1901 a council enlarged to 32 members and 23 committees held over five hundred meetings a year.

Initially sectarian bitterness was as evident as ever, reflected in the controversy that accompanied the building in 1882-3 of a large water tower, popularly known as 'Jumbo'. Planned to provide a 24-hour water supply to the whole town, it suffered initial problems. Partisan bickering, fully reported in an enlarged local press, erupted in the council. This upset a new generation of councillors who sat as city fathers, exemplified in the two party leaders: Wilson Marriage, the Quaker miller and Liberal, and Edwin Sanders, the Conservative owner of a large provisions merchant business: successful businessmen conducting the business of Colchester. Though both party men, they knew that the responsibility for providing services did not hinge on political majorities. Increasingly council affairs became more consensual, dignified and efficient as the borough debt rose to heights hitherto unimagined.

One consequence of a high profile council was a rise in civic ceremony, most obviously seen in the annual Oyster Feast where the current mayor entertained (at his own expense) the male elite of the town and guests of national importance arriving by special train from London: cabinet ministers, foreign dignitaries and members of the royal family. Colchester stopped for the day as the cavalcade of carriages made its way to High Street, through streets lined by crowds and brightly dressed garrison soldiers.

The fitting climax to this golden age of civic Colchester was the building of a lavish new town hall. Once again it had bi-partisan support in council; objections came only from below. Designed as a proud statement of Colchester's long history, it was really a civic cathedral with its stained glass windows, statues of secular 'saints' like Boudica and Thomas Lord Audley, and a tower reaching to heaven topped by St Helena, the ancient patron saint. With strict Victorian rectitude the building's many decorative features were paid for not by the ratepayers, but by gifts from local organisations and wealthy individuals. James Paxman, for example, financed the entire Victoria Tower.

111 On a grey morning in 1900 the new town hall reaches to heaven. The scaffolding of timber poles tied by rope required a specialist from the ship-building industry to check it each morning.

Victorian Colchester was proud of itself. Reviewing events in 1900, the influential *Essex County Standard* noted that hardly an organisation existed or building of note stood which had not been established that century.

112   Earnest Nonconformists attend the Pleasant Sunday Afternoon at Headgate Chapel where burning moral issues of the day were expounded to receptive audiences. Today the chapel is a theatre.

Even the castle was now more a museum than a ruin. Over the next 14 years new housing continued to spread, reflecting an unprecedented prosperity. Suburbs transformed the feel of Colchester as subtle variations of class took shape on the ground. Along Lexden Road gardens and large houses sustained by domestic servants provided the town's 'west end'. Hythe Hill with its picturesque mix of old houses and new industry provided an 'east end' of poverty, with a small resident middle class. Between them the spreading terraces of New Town, equipped from the outset with gas, mains water and sewers, provided homes for young upwardly mobile families, their respectability secured by privet hedge and lace curtain. Along Maldon Road clerks, shopkeepers and junior army officers lived a short distance from their Lexden Road 'betters'. The area north of High Street, extending along North Station Road, was more working class and popularly called 'the North'. As shopping absorbed more of the inner residential area, the old and increasingly decayed properties between North Hill and High Street were dubbed by antiquarians 'the Dutch Quarter', part of a growing tendency (as with the new town hall) to anchor the town's new self-confidence in its long history.

Of course, aspects of Colchester's past were still controversial, particularly if involving royalty or religion. Keen Liberals regarded Oliver Cromwell as the greatest man who ever lived; learned Conservatives thought the execution of Lucas and Lisle to be murder. Colchester's Protestant martyrs, burnt by Queen Mary, were frequently exhumed by Evangelicals to attack their High Church opponents. Church-going remained a majority activity throughout Victorian Colchester and only latterly did the sharp divide between Anglicans and Nonconformists begin to soften. A few clergy and pastors with powerful personalities, such as Joseph Herrick at Stockwell Chapel and Canon Irvine at St Mary's, were among the most influential and best-known men in the town. Religion sustained a male world

113 Colchester Town Football Club was the amateur predecessor to Colchester United. In 1912-13, their most successful season, the team exhibit the Border League Trophy, the Worthington Evans Cup, the South Essex League title vase and the East Anglian League champion's cup.

view. Deep concern was shown for the moral well-being of shop assistants and girls at the silk factory, but condescension towards the lower orders was not unknown. Businessmen exercised a paternalism which was both caring and autocratic. Children were seen but not heard, despite the large size of families. Muscular Christianity was fashionable.

Business partnerships, marriages and charitable initiatives, youth movements and temperance clubs were forged in church and chapel, along with political affiliation. Lion Walk Congregational Church supplied 19 Liberal mayors and 61 Liberal town councillors in 100 years. Sunday Schools processed thousands of children, providing women with one of the few public outlets for their energy and ability. Everyone learnt to read. An important arm of adult education was the Friends Adult School run by local Quakers. From 1812 to 1870 Anglican National Schools and Nonconformist schools of several kinds provided the bulk of day schools in the town.

When in 1871 the government introduced legislation requiring state schools to be built where none existed, Colchester's Anglicans made a dramatic effort to provide schools for every one of the town's 15 parishes. It was 20 years before Colchester adopted the act and built a new generation of 'Board' schools, which from 1902 came under council control. The grammar school, hitherto blighted by its Anglican status in a sectarian town, rose in 1900 from these ashes, under council care and its first secular headmaster Shaw Jeffery, to be a model of its kind. A large technical school, art school and girls' high school combined (today the Sixth Form College) was opened on North Hill in 1912.

Finally, religion played its part in a greater sense of British identity, indeed British destiny. The strident celebrations in Colchester of the Relief of Mafeking in 1900, with streets full of celebrating people and a triumphalist procession, were echoed in towns all over Essex, in fact all over England. Colchester might be

114 Market Day in High Street, 1905. A new tram flanks carrier carts from local villages; J. Sainsbury's have acquired an old family store.

a world unto itself but, as events in the new century were to show, its citizens already had wider horizons.

In 1914 Colchester High Street was alive with people, horses and carts, bicycles, frequent trams, three bus services, several steam wagons, and cars and vans in such numbers as to cause regular accidents. Since 1912 several aeroplanes had landed on the outskirts of the town. There were 40 places of worship (some of which held daily services), two cinemas and two theatres, including the lavish new Hippodrome where Charlie Chaplin and Marie Lloyd had both recently appeared. Two or three pubs ran their own 'music hall' and others tolerated

spontaneous singing. Many shops had electric lighting or took it as a power source. The town boasted over fifty football teams, not counting the many school elevens, and ran two or three leagues, including one for the beneficiaries of Thursday early closing. Cup matches could attract crowds of 3,000. This pen picture could be greatly extended, but serves to demonstrate that activities familiar to Colchester residents in the year 2000, would, apart from the horses and carts, have amazed residents of 1830. And Colchester was now a town of good government and good drains. This is a measure of the change in the period covered by this chapter.

Nine
War, Depression, War
1914-45

The First World War took Colchester by surprise. The first ever Essex cricket week had just been a success, with a win against Worcestershire in Castle Park. The August bank holiday had drawn a record 30,000 'excursionists' to Clacton, mostly by train, though newly acquired motorcycles were evident on the roads. Most locals firms were closed for the long weekend.

'The last seven days are like an incredible and detestable dream', declared the *Essex County Standard*, as war clouds blew up from nowhere. Reality, however, soon registered in a garrison town. Regular troops marched off; territorials joined the colours; soldiers were everywhere. There was a run on food at the shops, as the price of Marriage's flour rose by eight shillings a sack. Horses were commandeered in hundreds, just when harvest was beginning. One local woman shot her last two horses, when the others were taken away. More serious was the effect on those local factories with export business, as markets in Europe closed. Controls on transport and material soon caused tailoring firms to work half-time. Even the engineers, many of whose men, reservists, had joined the Essex Regiment, could not find enough work, though Paxman's were soon busy with secret Admiralty work, building paravanes to be towed by ships into minefields.

Shops were rather more fortunate. Colchester Garrison was earmarked to train a large part of Kitchener's Army, recruited by page-sized posters in all the local papers. In less than a month they arrived, many from London, with no uniforms or weapons, not knowing how to march. Billeted in houses all over Colchester, they were remembered as 'nice boys', sleeping in the front room and sharing meals with the family. As more and more came, huts, tents,

115 Autumn 1914: a photo opportunity for Kitchener recruits complete with their mugs and a benign sergeant major.

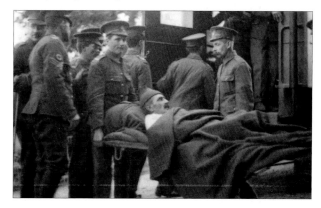

116 A wounded soldier being transferred to an ambulance outside St Botolph's Station.

117   Queuing for potatoes at St Botolph's Corner in 1917.

even warehouses, were requisitioned to put them up. By September there were 20,000 in the town. At times in the following four years there were 40,000, equalling the civilian population. Soldiers spent their money at a

118   Colchester 1918: local schoolteachers writing out ration cards in the Moot Hall.

famous rate. Even the trams made a profit, allowing any soldier in uniform to travel any distance for 1d. And feeding thousands of horses was good business too.

All over Colchester clubs sprang up, particularly in churches, to keep the men entertained. The big appeal was to be indoors. The borough had decided to close pubs for the sale of alcohol at 9 p.m. 'to prevent soldiers rendering themselves unfit for training'. A booklet published by the council listed 35 such clubs. Then the first wounded arrived. By winter 1915 the arrival of hundreds of wounded at St Botolph's Station was a routine Colchester event, as hospital capacity in the borough expanded: Hamilton Road School, several large huts and converted private houses joined the Military Hospital and the hospital on Lexden Road. Things were made worse by a serious outbreak of meningitis and the devastating flu epidemic at the end of the war. By 1918 Colchester was nursing over three thousand sick and wounded.

Recruitment of Colchester men meanwhile went on apace, especially of, the paper noted, 'sturdy young men from the country'. In reality about 25 per cent were rejected as unfit. Nor was local recruitment (1,532 by mid-1915) that impressive. Partly, of course, the concept of 'reserved occupation' stemmed the flow from the factories, but partly, as one critic candidly put it, 'there is no glamour to the army in Colchester and wages are good at Paxman's'. Far more men enlisted with the introduction of conscription. This in turn required the Colchester Military Tribunal to adjudicate on those asking for exemption, usually on commercial grounds. By 1916 many local businesses were running with a fraction of their former manpower, dependent on older men exempt from service. Benjamin Cant Ltd., rose growers (and by now vegetable growers too), had lost 40 of their 66 men, Daniell's Breweries 65 out of 90 men. Not all these vacancies could be filled by women or boys. Women did ease the manpower crisis in agriculture and the tramways recruited 14 much-photographed conductresses, but women were not considered for the decimated borough police force until 1918.

Middle-class women, rather than earn money, devoted themselves to good works. Mrs Coats Hutton, a wartime mayoress, marshalled them in their hundreds. The borough social club for troops, the WMCA, the 'basket fund', the Free Buffet for the Wounded: all had many helpers and large committees. The War Work Depot in one year provided the military hospital with 10,423 surgical swabs, 22,488 rolled bandages, 2,972 other bandages, 92 stump bandages, 1,248 plugs, 443 theatre towels, 414 eye pads, 120 helpless case shirts … the list goes on for several lines. That these items were made by housewives

in their spare time is matched by the fact that they were all apparently needed.

Far more relevant to the war effort was the rising level of employment in the town as the nation got onto a war footing. Clothing factories worked long, long hours on military contracts. Decades later women still remembered the tough stitching of thick serge greatcoats. From 1916 the engineering factories were busy with munitions: shells, mines, depth charges, quick-firing guns. Mumford's made pumps, marine engines and feed water regulators for warships. Paxman's made a bewildering range of products: from the 'otters' which cut mine cables to parts for tanks, ships, submarines, lorries, refrigeration plants and even aeroplanes. Both firms saw their works enlarged, quantities of new equipment fitted and production line techniques learnt. Large numbers of women worked on shells; profits, even after the deduction of 'excess profit tax', were the highest both firms had ever made. The smaller engineering firms were equally busy and doubtless equally profitable.

There was money in people's pockets, even if inflation halved its purchasing power, and increasing government control of prices and profits helped the majority. It mattered whether billeting pay was 2s. 6d. or 2s. 9d. a day, but no one marched about it. Most Colchester people had never had it so good. Normal life had changed in many ways. The new Central School in Hamilton Road became a hospital; the old Corn Exchange became the Recruiting Office; Layer Road Football Ground was handed over to the military for drill. But the real headquarters of Colchester was the town hall, as directives on all matters flew down from Whitehall. In one sense, as Alderman Benham pointed out, Colchester was under martial law. But if London dictated, mayor and corporation implemented.

There were 100 special constables to be appointed, National Savings drives to be promoted and sale of War Bonds targets to be met (they never were). The Borough Tribunal had to be cross-party and cross-class, though the Independent Labour Party, opposed to war, became almost a prescribed organisation. There were rats to be caught; sparrows and rooks to be slaughtered in the name of agricultural production; paper to be collected and blackberries to be picked in hundreds of tons by schoolchildren on a set weekend. New territory was entered with the control of civilian movement, and, as the war ground on, control over limited food reserves. Potatoes were grown in unlikely places. By constant effort 2,200 allotments covering 200 acres were established. Those digging vegetables on a still Sunday morning could hear guns on the Western Front: they were nearer than Lincoln.

Above all, the borough's Food Control Committee became responsible for a host of measures limiting supplies and prices. By late 1917 queues for food were becoming so contentious that rationing came as a relief. All Colchester schools were closed for a week and 180 elementary school teachers, nearly all women, sat in the town hall handwriting 80,000 ration cards which were distributed to 10,000 households by boy scouts. Such local action epitomised 'the nation at war' in microcosm. Long Victorian conditioning had taught Colchester's middle classes to lead and the rest to follow, whatever their private thoughts. What was happening at home was the civilian equivalent of the officer class leading their men 'over the top'.

At times it felt like war. In 1917 the mayor of Colchester, backed by a posse of 'specials', confronted a crowd of 2,000 besieging delivery vans in Long Wyre Street. All Colchester's margarine came from the Maypole Dairy. Citing the Defence of the Realm Act, the mayor commandeered two tons, announcing it would be sold at fixed prices in 12 centres by the Food Control Committee. Partly the mayor

acted because he had heard that foundrymen at Paxman's had threatened to strike if their wives (and children) had to queue in the manner of the past few weeks. This was Colchester in 1917, not St Petersburg.

There were, of course, no Oyster Feasts or local elections held, though an energetic munitions workers' football league was a great success. Vacancies on the council were filled by co-option, resulting in the town's first two woman councillors: one Labour, one Conservative. Blackout was another novelty, slowly, even grudgingly, introduced, until pillar boxes needed white stripes to be seen and trams were stopped lest their sparks should be noticed on high. For this war provided a new hazard: air raids. In February 1915 a German bomb fell on a garden in Butt Road, broke several windows, killed a thrush and wrecked a baby's pram. Postcards of a soldier guarding the garden sold like hot cakes. Lady Colebrooke generously replaced the pram. More common than aeroplanes were Zeppelins heading towards London. On one day in 1915 five could be seen over Colchester at once; perhaps they were lost. When one ditched at Great Wigborough half of Colchester went to look at it. Increasing press censorship meant that later bombs went unmentioned.

Despite several spy scares there wasn't the need for boy scouts to guard bridges and watch telegraph wires, though it helped them feel useful. Indeed Colchester, with its memories of the 1856 German Legion, never indulged in racial attacks. Cards were, however, issued to all households detailing instruction of where to march to in the event of invasion. The town hall basement was kept full of tinned food for people fleeing from Clacton. Because of Colchester's strategic importance, King George V visited the district several times, notably to inspect a military bridge, built between Wivenhoe and Rowhedge, which upset local barge owners.

119 Peace celebrations in 1919: soldiers march down St Botolph's Street. Note the early bus in Osborne Street.

Churches were very busy. Large open-air services marked each anniversary of the outbreak of war. 1916 opened with a Day of Penitence and self-denial, followed by a Service of Intercession. The great German offensive of 1918, launched to win the war before the Americans arrived, forced Colchester to think the unthinkable. Being the garrison responsible for the defence of London, it received some alarming dispatches: 'Be prepared for invasion ... and if the grave hour ever comes that compels a surrender, let the enemy find Colchester a barren desert.' Hysteria, born of exhaustion, almost broke the stiff upper lips. Colchester's M.P., Laming Worthington Evans, was now a junior minister. Sending his apologies for missing a meeting in the town he cabled: 'The crisis is upon

us! A crisis in which brute force is seeking to dominate the world! In order to foil this attempt the Empire is demanding complete and ungrudging sacrifice!'

The Armistice almost caught Colchester by surprise. The town council was actually in session. They rose to their feet and sang the National Anthem, while the mayor addressed the town from his balcony: 'This is the greatest day in the world's history ... fellow citizens, rejoice with me.' They did. For three days. But even here there were mixed messages. The press describes munitions workers marching round the streets in a spontaneous act of celebration. From oral testimony we know that this was stage-managed by trade unions and concluded with a soviet-style harangue from the balcony of the Labour Club at St Botolph's Corner

120 Colchester High Street in the 1920s: still a quiet market town. The cab rank of 1862 is now a taxi rank.

about the need for solidarity in the industrial war about to begin.

'The four years of the Great War were perhaps the most memorable in the long and eventful history of ... Colchester.' So begins Colchester's memorial booklet. This and the emotional scenes at the unveiling of the war memorial in 1923 tell us much. So do two statistics. Relative to its population Colchester's 1,248 war dead greatly exceeded that of any other town in the eastern counties: 21 per cent of those grammar school boys who enlisted were killed. And the flu epidemic killed yet more. There can have been few homes

untouched. Particularly hit were a number of leading families, pillars of the Victorian establishment, whose sons and heirs did not come home. Colchester's 1921 population was actually smaller than that of 1911. In part this was due to a reduced garrison, but only in part.

The Depression

Nor were the years which followed 'business as usual'. As a market economy returned, inflation fuelled labour unrest. Tram workers struck for higher wages. A grumpy council granted them: they had been waiting the outcome of national negotiations. Paxman's were hamstrung by a strike of foundrymen: another national strike. The management was quite glad: their order books were empty. Busy with government munitions (and the government always paid), engineering firms with world markets now had to find overseas agents, fight off American competition and cope with the disintegration of central and eastern Europe. Clothing firms lost overseas orders; printers could not get enough paper.

Demobilisation sent all the soldiers home. Colchester by 1921 had 13 per cent unemployment. Included in the depression was agriculture. Colchester was still, on a Saturday, a farmer's town. With the livestock market in the morning and the corn exchange in the afternoon, farmers ate large lunches in the *George Inn*: red-faced men in tweed jackets, discussing their misfortunes.

With government grants, Colchester provided some relief work: building roads and extending Hythe Quay. Rates more than doubled. Then the Wall Street Crash shattered the world economy. One casualty was the engineering conglomerate which Paxman's had joined. Though still profitable itself, it hosted a receiver. The managing director, Percy Sanders (son of Edwin), paid the men out of his own pocket. Stanford's closed in 1924; Mumford's in 1932.

121   East Bridge, on the main road to Ipswich and Clacton, being widened as part of local relief work in 1927.

122   The new Colchester Bypass was built with the aid of a small electric railway. Here it passes through The Glen (today by Glen Avenue).

123   Britain's first two-hinged arch bridge, constructed over the River Colne, also provided the town with a public bathing pool.

The Britannia Company constantly flirted with insolvency. Engineering, Colchester's largest industry, was in crisis, as local unemployment touched 20 per cent.

Some relief was provided by the building of a bypass, opened in 1933. Crouch Street – Head Street – High Street – East Bridge still formed the main road from London to Norwich, and from London to the coastal resorts. Bank holidays produced serious traffic jams. A handful of Welsh miners were imported (a 'distressed area') and government funding

was secured. Up to 300 men a week, many of them skilled engineers, used picks and shovels, one mechanical excavator and a small light railway to build a 3¾-mile road from Lexden to Elmstead Road. Over 750 new trees helped fringe an 'Avenue of Remembrance.' In theory the men worked for six weeks and were then replaced, thereby becoming eligible for unemployment pay. Over one thousand were thus put to work. It was a remarkable undertaking and included Britain's first two-hinged arch bridge, crossing the river, plus

124 Increased leisure: girls from Hyam's factory on a 1920s works outing to London Zoo.

a second crossing the railway, designed by a 24-year-old with no prior experience. In 2000 the 'bypass' still coped with the pounding of 21st-century juggernauts.

Talk of increased road traffic, which included 30 motor buses bringing shoppers to Colchester, reminds us that the 1930s saw shorter working hours and improved living standards, helped by the building of 3,383 inter-war houses. These included 1,242 council houses on small estates at Mile End, Lexden, Old Heath and, above all, 'the White City', as the estate east of Ipswich Road was called. Full employment also marked the later 1930s as rearmament kept Colchester's factories busy. 'Old' industry, indeed, enjoyed an Indian summer. Paxman's were expanding their sales of diesel engines; Woods, manufacturers of fans, relocated to a new factory north of the river valley; Mason's, makers of engineering blueprints and a range of office equipment,

relocated to the new bypass, almost opposite the borough's new fire station. The old clothing factories were busy, and soon making uniforms again. The army bought more land to the south of the town, built new barracks and maintained its large presence.

Though grants in aid were a growing phenomenon, the town hall still reigned supreme. Colchester people did not moan about 'the government', but about 'the council'. In retrospect the 1930s stand at the end of a golden age of local government stretching from about 1880: borough councils high in esteem and big in responsibility. Aldermen were long-serving men of moment; one, indeed, was a woman. Fifty years saw only two town clerks, three museum curators, three chief constables and lots of promotion from within. Put another way, Colchester was distinctly provincial. Most Colcestrians had been born in the town; you

125 Hythe 1930: men in overcoats with large shovels have just unloaded a Tyneside collier bringing coal for the gas works.

met people in High Street you went to school with. Freemasonry was strong. It was a face-to-face town whose elite still aspired to serve on the council. This now included the leaders of Colchester's large labour movement, to whom seats at the table were only grudgingly granted: indeed, they had to storm the citadel.

The 1918 general election saw not only a 130 per cent increase in the electorate, but the absorption of the whole Lexden & Winstree Hundred into the constituency. Such a seat could never be won by the Liberals and, with David Lloyd George standing as a coalition Prime Minister, Labour ran its first Parliamentary candidate, backed by the Colchester & East Essex Co-op, hitherto the 'labour' arm of the Liberal Party. Leading Liberals were prominent at the victory celebration of Worthington Evans, the Conservative coalition candidate, and after 1919 the two old parties had little to divide them and much to unite them in suspicion of socialism and the class-based agenda of Labour. On paper, throughout the inter-war period,

the council was 'hung' between the three parties. In practice, Conservatives and Liberals conspired not to oppose one another if this led to a Labour victory. They also continued to share out the aldermanic seats (four each) and alternated the mayoralty between them. At a council meeting in January 1926 Labour pursued a day-long filibuster, until granted an aldermanic seat and three-way participation in the mayoralty.

Though trade union leadership was undoubtedly embattled, it is less clear how far the General Strike divided Colchester in 1926. Most local businesses were family-owned (the railways were a notable exception) and their management were not lacking in inter-personal skills. Indeed, without it, they would not have lasted very long. The National Strike was a national event. Union members were out in sympathy with the miners, not necessarily in hostility to their employers.

The town council, of course, was a major employer, who replaced its trams with a fleet

126 The newly-completed Turner Village in 1935.

of buses, built three more schools, tarred all the main streets, installed a new main sewer, carved out a bus park and a car park, roofed the castle to extend the museum, found new water supplies and employed a remarkable police force. Colonel Stockwell, the chief constable, systematically recruited army athletes and boxing champions to his force. This not only helped subdue 'the North Gang', more terrible for its self-image than its crimes, but led to a celebrated boxing match in 1936, when Colchester lost to the German police champions from Stuttgart.

In reality Colchester was now a quiet and sober town. Children played safely in the streets; indeed, with a falling birth rate and improved education, children had a good decade. As late as 1915 over thirty per cent of Colchester's children had still had head or body lice. Petty larceny was now Colchester's worst crime; murder or political corruption was unknown, though a small but active branch of the British Union of Fascists brought Sir Oswald Mosley to address a large meeting in the Albert Hall, shortly before it became home to the Colchester Repertory Theatre.

Undoubtedly the most impressive arm of the borough was its electricity department. An early post-war decision was made to build a large new AC generating station at the Hythe. Opened in 1927 and extended in 1930, its

lines carried power not just to Colchester but to over 350 square miles of the surrounding rural area. Indeed, Colchester was regarded in London as an exemplar at supplying power to rural areas, eventually linked to other main stations at Norwich and Barking. So great was the progress that the loss of the trams was barely noticed. Domestic water heating was introduced and 5,500 electric cookers were installed by its 22 vans by 1935. So futuristic an achievement was epitomised by Colchester's 'Eiffel tower', a 220-foot-high pylon carrying power at 11,000 volts over the Hythe to Rowhedge. The service also made a profit. Only the establishment of the National Grid ended this Colchester success story.

Other 'new' industries saw the building of a large district telephone exchange in Stockwell Street and the opening of Colchester's third cinema, the Regal (later Odeon), a 'dream palace' built in Crouch Street, complete with restaurant and Wurlitzer organ. Two-thirds of a new public library was built facing the new car park (a compromise compelled by the Ratepayers' Party) though the unused bricks were kept until 1968. More downmarket was the dog-racing track at Land Lane. Cricket and football were played in leagues by schools, works' teams and neighbourhood clubs. The Colchester Town team performed modestly in the Spartan League, paying 'expenses' to young West Ham players. Finally in 1938 Colchester United was born as a fully professional club. The Colchester Carnival Procession was an inter-war innovation, letting the hair down slightly to raise money for the Colchester & Essex Hospital, still 'sustained by voluntary contributions'.

Perhaps the most remarkable inter-war building achievement was Turner Village. Over the previous century Colchester had become a major centre for those with mental disabilities. This began in 1850 when the failed *Victoria Hotel* at North Station evolved into Essex

Hall, only the second such institution in Britain for those with special needs, labelled in the vocabulary of the day as The Eastern Counties Asylum for Idiots. It served and was funded by Norfolk, Suffolk, Cambridgeshire and Essex. From an initial hundred or so residents the complex grew by addition and buildings acquired elsewhere to become the Royal Eastern Counties Institution with, by 1918, accommodation for 630 inmates. Several members of the Turner family worked here, notably the secretary, J.J.C. Turner. Essex Hall always sought to provide occupation and recreation appropriate for its inmates.

Turner's son, Douglas, a qualified doctor, became resident medical officer and the driving force after the war. Inmates now included a growing number of 'moral imbeciles', declared by their parents and a doctor to be 'promiscuous'. Douglas Turner worked to build a new residential facility, opened in 1935 and called Turner Village. Set in 100 acres, it housed all male residents (the female remained at Essex Hall) in eight large 'villas', segregated by 'grades', reflecting both the best and worst of contemporary practice. There was a security fence, an authoritarian control over all the residents did and tranquillisers for the recalcitrant. But there was also a commitment to provide activities like a Boy Scout and Girl Guide troop and a wide range of productive work, including a formidable output of rugs, clothes, boots and farm produce. By 1938 Essex Hall & Turner Village housed 1,900 residents.

Mile End also housed 'Severall's', a county council psychiatric hospital with over two thousand in-patients, which opened in 1913. With 300 acres of land and buildings, its own farm, chapel, laundry, electricity supply, kitchens, maintenance workshops, cricket pitch and the biggest dance hall for miles around, Severall's was very large. It was also self-contained and ringed by a security fence which was both physical and psychological. Families who came from the North of England to help with construction stayed on to train as staff. To Mile End's rural citizens Severall's was another world from which patients 'escaped'. To the people of Colchester it became a blind spot in their self image: Colchester was home to one of the largest garrisons in Britain, but not to three large mental institutions with 4,000 residents.

The Second World War
The Second World War did not take Colchester by surprise. Most people listened apprehensively to Chamberlain's radio broadcast. Others were down at St Botolph's Station coping with the arrival over three days of 12,000 London evacuees: pregnant women, mothers with babies, children. Most of these were disbursed into surrounding villages; Colchester was fulfilling its traditional role, billeting soldiers. No one questioned universal conscription. Sandbags were filled with vigour, the spares piled up outside the town hall.

Territorials from the Essex Regiment spent the night in a Hythe warehouse before parading on the Culver Street Car Park outside the two-thirds library. This was promptly requisitioned, becoming the Food Control Office, an organisation planned, like evacuation and civil defence, a year in advance. From the outset the town accepted the disruption and discomfort of war: blackout, food rationing, fire watching and (for those who had them) the loss of private cars. After all, there was a public memory. A generation had grown up listening to stories of the last war. Some indeed had served. In Colchester the town clerk, the police chief, the fire chief and several senior members of the town council had held office. Percy Sanders (of Paxman's) duly became mayor from 1939 to 1943. Once more 100 specials were enrolled, starting with those who had volunteered during the 1926 strike. Once more boy scouts helped – issuing gas masks and erecting Morrison shelters in Colchester homes. Once more over 40,000 ration books were issued, over half

127 These four cheerful Colchester evacuees have just arrived at Burton-on-Trent in 1940.

Colchester's households registering with the Colchester & East Essex Co-op, evidence of its extraordinary importance in the district. Once more allotments were dug for victory and Cant's roses were replaced by vegetables.

History, however, never quite repeats itself. Civilian bombing was far more serious this time: hence the gas masks and the shelters both public and domestic, though the former, in Colchester, were not used very much. Hence the 960 members of the Royal Observer Corps linked to the centre on Lexden Road, the 800 local air-raid wardens, the 7,570 street-based fire watchers, the 300 men manning the AA battery on the Abbey Field after a full day's work. In due course even more men served in 'Dad's Army', the Home Guard. This, of

course, was after the fall of France in June 1940 which triggered the inevitable fear of invasion. An outer defence line for London actually ran through Colchester. Anti-tank ditches were dug and linked with the Iron-Age dykes extended by the Romans after AD 43.

Fear of invasion turned Colchester from a reception area into an evacuation area, though it was September before 13,000 children, some 60 per cent of the borough's total, were taken by train to Kettering, Wellingborough, Stoke and Burton-on-Trent. Neither parents nor children knew where they were going, but the few able to telephone on arrival ensured that the word spread. Though most children had to spend their first night in a local school, this evacuation seems to have worked relatively smoothly and few horror stories emerged of unsuitable accommodation. The real heroes were the often young schoolteachers travelling with the children, finding themselves surrogate parents, community negotiators and teachers in equal measure. Children remembered, ever after, half-day schooling and the smell of Marmite and brewing beer which Burton exuded.

Much as the London evacuees to Colchester had drifted home after the first few months, so too most Colchester evacuees returned during the first winter, a process accelerated when two Lexden children were tragically killed by a random bomb at Rushden. Returning seems to have been the product of spontaneous parent power, often discussed outside school gates and arranged among those few having motor transport to bring the children home. Headteachers had to cope for several months with schools split half and half between Colchester and the Midlands.

The first explosive German bomb fell on Colchester in August 1940. There were to be at least 1,800 more, not counting thousands of incendiaries. Nevertheless, it does seem that no combined air raid was ever directed against Colchester, a major garrison town. All bombs seem to have been of the 'tip and run' variety, single planes offloading their explosives, usually on their return from raids over London. Colchester got off lightly compared with Ipswich or Chelmsford. Some 54 civilians were killed, 38 by one direct hit on a geriatric ward at Severall's Hospital. Fifty houses were destroyed, 1,750 damaged. By far the biggest bonfire was caused by the dropping of at least 1,400 incendiaries, mostly on St Botolph's Corner, at midnight on 23 February 1944. The blaze could be seen at Bury St Edmunds. Some 19 properties were destroyed, including two clothing factories, 11 shops and part of the Britannia Works where Paxman engines were being assembled. Jumbo the watertower ran dry as 500 firemen pumped two million

128 Exhausted fireman survey the chaos at St Botolph's Corner in the cold light of dawn, following the massive midnight incendiary blaze of 23 February 1944.

gallons through 70 appliances. Colchester was also fortunate, late in the war, in receiving no real direct hits from V1 'doodle bugs' or V2 rockets, though the former were seen in some numbers.

As a garrison town, Colchester was full of troops. This included numbers of noisy Australians, Czechs, Indians and, eventually, Americans from the many air bases in the north of Essex. As elsewhere, they supplied chocolate to children, nylons to girlfriends and invites to celebrated dances. Their legacy included some unwanted pregnancies and a reputation for generosity. The SAS trained at Wivenhoe Park and the Timber Corps of the Women's Land Army cut pit props at Langham. There were many Land Army girls in North Essex, some in hostels in Colchester, part of the conscription of women which began in 1941, when those under thirty had to choose between the services and war work.

Those who chose war work in Colchester once more took up engineering. Even before war began Paxman's were making submarine mines and paravanes. During the war, with a workforce rising to 2,300 (over 700 were women) their output of 7,000 high-speed diesel engines was the largest in Britain. These drove tanks, submarines and AA batteries. A special engine was designed for North African and

129 Women assembling Paxman TP Vee-engines at the Britannia Works in 1944.

D-Day landing craft, broken down into small parts, provided by 550 suppliers nationwide and assembled at the reconditioned Britannia Works, mainly by 'unskilled' female labour. Elsewhere women formed half of Woods' workforce of 800, manufacturing fans and electric motors at five factories in Colchester and one in Cambridge. The Colchester Lathe Company and Brackett's were other large employers. The clothing factories employed 1,600 making uniforms; the Anglo-Italian Silk Company in North Station Road made parachute material. Mason's 800 staff made special paper in extraordinary quantities for photo-reconnaissance and pioneered the development of photocopying. A notable part was played by the revival of shipbuilding at Rowhedge and Wivenhoe, making steel tankers, motor torpedo boats and minesweepers built entirely in wood. Numbers of women worked here too.

Colchester gave generously to the many savings campaigns; this was a 'peoples' war' and none doubted its justice. It ended with the customary street parties and an earnest determination to build a brighter tomorrow. In pursuit of total war the nation had been directed by central government to a quite unprecedented extent. This was to continue. Colchester's war output was one cog in a state-controlled wheel. Cinemas, newspapers and the BBC sustained a sense of national identity in every sitting room. This included the sitting rooms of Colchester whose fire service was a National Fire Service, whose W.V.S., Home Guard and Royal Observer Corps were subject to wider national bodies. The War Agricultural Committee was a county body. There was an Eastern Region Commissioner.

Because VE Day and VJ Day were distinct events, because the men came back slowly, post-war reconstruction and the legacy of war became merged. Italian prisoners-of-war dug the drainage for Colchester's post-war housing. German prisoners-of-war at Berechurch Camp trained as Catholic priests. In due course Colchester's town hall war memorial added 239 names to its list, as husbands and wives, often half-strangers, met again and shivered in the bitter winter of 1945.

Ten

As Far as the Eye can See
1945-2000

Between 1945 and 2000 the population of the Colchester urban area almost doubled from perhaps 54,000 to 102,000. Nor does this include those in Tiptree, Wivenhoe, Mersea and the villages which now form part of the administrative district. In the same period over 30,000 new houses were built, against a starting total of about 14,200. Such spectacular suburban growth put increased strain on the town's historic core as planners juggled with competing demands to maximise its retail potential or retain its period charm. The mass ownership of cars also made demands. If two words can mark the period covered by this chapter they are 'unprecedented expansion'.

In 1945 the need for new housing was self-evident: none had been built for six years. There were three-bedroom homes housing 12 people. There was a waiting list of 1,100 for 37 'pre-fabs' being built by the Ministry of Works in Tufnell Way. But skills and materials were desperately scarce and permission to build was only grudgingly granted. Complaints about 'red tape' peppered the deliberations of the town council. In their enthusiasm the borough badly overspent on building council houses at Barn Hall with a 300-strong direct labour force. Fifty 'Orlitt' houses assembled from kits were another unhappy expedient. By January 1949 only 262 houses had been finished, builders were working a five-day week and the waiting list was 2,170. A group of squatters settled in Nissen huts on the decommissioned Boxted aerodrome. The local authority threatened to evict them and

cut off their water supply, yet within months changed tack, took over the huts and charged a low rent. By 1954 over 200 families were living on former airfields at Boxted, Birch, Bures, Wakes Colne and Wormingford.

Ideology compounded the challenge. In 1945 Colchester acquired its first Labour M.P. and the Labour Party secured control of Colchester council, but only just. Wafer-thin majorities and the decline of the Liberal Party saw the chair of the housing committee switch from side to side as the rival merits of direct labour and 'private enterprise' were preached. Ideology and central government also eroded the borough's responsibilities. The borough police force and fire service both came under county control. Even town planning became a

130 Orlitt houses under construction in 1946. The site foreman stands with, third from left, Colchester's Labour M.P. Charles Smith and his former agent, Jack Andrews, second left, now Chairman of the Borough Housing Committee.

131 The Commons in 1959, a new estate built by W.A. Hills & Sons, rising affluence being more evident in television aerials than private cars.

county responsibility, as did education, despite the establishment in the town of a North-East Essex Divisional Office. River Boards took over the Colne; the Inland Revenue took over rating valuation. The National Health Service put the hospitals under regional boards and nationalisation deprived the borough of its electricity department, valued at £2½ million, but taken with only £50,000 compensation. For a time it looked as if the buses (currently making a profit) would go too; water, of course, did later.

The erosion of old powers helped discourage many from seeking municipal office. The old families faded, the new captains of industry demurred. The characteristic background of new councillors was as strong party activists. In the process their social profile edged downwards. The electorate, or the 45 per cent who bothered to vote, increasingly treated local elections as a referendum on Westminster politics. Then there was the power of county hall, regarded by a section of the council as 'the enemy'. In taking over education, Essex County Council had become a colossus. Its budget, now measured in millions, absorbed most of Colchester's rates. Its atmosphere was often sharply political, power changing sides at almost each election.

Housing continued to dominate council affairs as Conservatives won back control in the1950s. Shrub End and Monkwick yielded 1,250 units each (a unit can be a house or a flat); the Army built the 1000-plus Montgomery estate; and private estates blossomed at Prettygate and Home Farm. Colchester had no real slums to demolish and was spared new high-rise towerblock housing, as, from the late 1950s, the vast Greenstead Estate spread. Once earmarked by Essex County Council for London overspill population this, with St John's beside it, grew to be one of the largest council estates in the country with (eventually) 3,800 units. Many of the new houses were taken by in-migrants, the majority coming from elsewhere in south-east Britain. The electrification of the railway line reduced travelling time to London to one hour and commuting began to increase. Even as Colchester residents travelled away to work, a greater number from the surrounding area, notably Clacton, Braintree and Tiptree, travelled in to Colchester each day. They also, of course, came to shop.

During the 1960s, a decade of dramatic population growth, Colchester began to lose its East Anglian remoteness, becoming part of 'Estuary England'. Newcomers outnumbered natives, particularly among professionals and managers, who soon had stories to tell of Colchester's whimsical ways and archaic industrial practices: some Paxman workshops had earth floors; some rural workers no electricity. A new town clerk, Norman Catchpole, appointed in 1947, worked on his first day until 7 p.m. and came downstairs to find his entire staff waiting for permission to go home. Housewives no longer knew every street in Colchester. The local accent died. So did a once robust Protestantism.

Suburban living hastened this decline. Several town-centre churches were redundant. Under a 1954 reorganisation the Church of England opted to sell the mainly Victorian

132 A pivotal High Street moment as demolition begins in January 1955 on the Victorian spire of St Nicholas Church. High Street traffic is still two-way and Kent & Blaxill still trade in their historic premises. All this will change.

133 A streetscape is transformed in 1972 as a footbridge spans historic Queen Street in the shadow of the new Keddie's Store to enable motorists to cross in freedom from their new multi-storey car park.

134 Throughout the late 20th century controversy raged over the desirability of retaining or moving the traditional market stalls, erected every Saturday in High Street since medieval times.

gothic St Nicholas, one of the last churches of the great Sir George Gilbert Scott. It was a prime High Street site reckoned to fetch £40,000. At a famous auction in the *Red Lion* it sold to London developers for £88,000. The church was demolished and in its place stood a new flagship Co-op store, proclaiming on its opening day the sale of Co-op television sets. Colchester's retail property boom was born.

Town-Centre Development

The post-war emphasis on housing had left little time for new shopping development. The town was full of small retail properties, bought up a generation earlier for investment potential and making a sparse living for traditional shopkeepers. The *Red Lion* sale taught many a small owner with little of their 50-year lease remaining, that the time had come to sell. They were sitting on a gold mine. No one exploited the new potential better than Robin Tomkins, founder of Frincon Holdings, who built tower blocks in St Peter's Street, the Centurion House shops in St John's Street and the ultra-modern Queen Street-Kingsway development accommodating the Southend retailers, Keddie's.

Matters were made more dramatic by the increase in car ownership. In 1963 the one-way street system was introduced to High Street, and Kent & Blaxill pioneered the future by moving to an out-of-town site. In 1962 a Colchester Redevelopment Plan proposed a dual carriageway ring road, six new car parks catering for 3,800 cars, and a large 'comprehensive development area' south of Culver Street. Subsequently refined by the borough's own planning department, which grew dramatically in the following decades, this formed a blueprint for the next 25 years. What Hitler had spared the borough council was about to destroy.

For a suburban-living town this represented a challenge to the very concept of Colchester. 'Colchester' came to mean the downtown historic core. Getting there by car soon became

135 The 1974 'hole in the ground', created to enable the new Lion Walk Precinct to be serviced by underground access.

as important as finding supermarkets or night clubs when you arrived. Newcomers and natives were torn between the prospect of something new and exciting within their midst and the disturbing demolition, not just of old landmarks, but of a historic, sometimes quaint, old town.

The formation in 1964 of the Civic Society, a gathering of the great and the good, gave this unease a focused respectability. Probably the greatest confrontation centred round the wilful destruction of the Regency assembly room in the *Cups Hotel*, next to the town hall.

136 The 'magic roundabout', where North Station Road met Cowdray Avenue, suffered countless traffic flow experiments as Colchester became famous for roundabout innovations. This is a 1972 version.

Part One of the 'comprehensive development' was the Lion Walk Precinct (1968-76). In the most expensive property deal in Colchester's history it became a joint Borough-Frincon project. Sir Frederick Gibberd, a leading national architect, designed the whole in brick, a shrewd decision when the nation was railing against 'concrete jungles'. Its most remarkable feature was to service the entire complex from underground, taking advantage of the fact that the town centre, inside the ancient walls, was up to seven metres higher than access outside. This involved breaching the Roman wall and bulldozing 2,000 years of archaeology, four metres deep and the size of two football pitches. This in turn prompted the largest archaeological dig in Colchester's history, its findings exciting considerable local interest.

The feeling of upheaval was enhanced by the almost simultaneous building of Southway, the first part of the dual carriageway ring road, slicing through Victorian developments and residential areas. A further dualling followed down Balkerne Hill and north towards the railway. By 1981 five multi-storey car parks built in a range of styles were in use. Cumulatively these projects demolished over 500 houses and scores of period buildings. Between 1968 and 1980 the commercial floor space in the central area increased by 45 per cent, but there was a 12 per cent decrease in the number of food shops. Shopping was increasingly dominated by chain stores seeking to impose their own image and house styles. The town's rateable value rose considerably.

Old Colchester, however, was not obliterated. The Dutch Quarter won an award for an enlightened restoration programme, enhanced over two decades by sensitive in-filling: at least north of High Street there were central area residents. The Lion Walk Precinct was integrated into historic areas like Trinity Street. The borough's new planning office increasingly compelled central area developers to retain attractive period facades, or design ones with period features, even if the rest of a site was rebuilt. The Co-op's redevelopment of one side of Long Wyre Street produced not a monolith, but a ranged set of buildings. The borough's new accommodation in Angle Court was housed, not in a high-rise 'politburo' as once proposed, but in architecture which replicated in breeze blocks the original historic townscape. In this way High Street has retained its late Victorian bravado, though Lion Walk dealt it a death blow as the town's premier shopping location.

Part Two of the 'comprehensive development' was the Culver Precinct, opened in 1987 after delays due to the economic recession of the 1980s. It looked a bit like Legoland but followed a similar pattern to Lion Walk: archaeological excavation, underground servicing via a breach in the Roman wall, and the search for a 'leading national retailer' to attract shoppers. Banishing cars to the basements secured that easy flow of humanity that has been the essence of town life for centuries. Debate about the size of the 'town square' this provided hardly seemed justified. Culver Square did not attract people in numbers for its own sake. Nor was the borough prepared to forsake the natural arena in front of the town hall, the home of civic ceremony for centuries. What the town square debate showed was the passionate wish for downtown Colchester to have style as well as bargains.

All this concern with shopping illustrates how Colchester was moving, like the nation, from post-war austerity to post-modern affluence. Washing machines, central heating and cars became universal. Colchester teenagers gyrated in hula hoops in 1958 and bought Beatles records in armfuls in 1964. Sainsbury's opened their second largest self-service store in Britain in Colchester's Kingsway. Along with affluence came radicalism, itself one aspect of a 'youth culture' by which sociology, the new religion, termed the assault on old world deference, once so characteristic of the town. Nowhere was this new world disorder more strident than at the University of Essex, opened in a modest way in 1964. Its siting at Wivenhoe Park in the green-field outskirts of the town was a rare victory over Chelmsford, which was now expanding faster, as the home of County Hall and, since 1907, the diocese of Essex.

Colchester was at first unsure how to treat the new academic kingdom without its gates, with its dramatic concrete rafts and high-rise black brick towers. Uncertainty became misgiving as the campus became a major centre of student unrest, increasingly in the media spotlight. To the radical young it became a Mecca, to Colchester police the source of unlikely tales. But as time passed so did student unrest, and town and gown grew closer. Not only was the university a major source of employment but it harnessed the frontiers of knowledge to the borough's dislike of the 'Essex girl' image with which the county was stigmatised in the 1990s. As the academic reputation of the university rose, it became a useful status symbol.

More significantly for the feel of the town, the large intake of overseas students and staff provided, like the hospitals and other training institutions, an element of multi-culturalism which the town otherwise lacked. Colchester did not experience a significant influx of Afro-Caribbean or Asian immigration, though time and in-migration had changed the overall picture by the year 2000. Outstanding sports facilities, academic and social events made open to the public, and support for local initiatives, all now added to the university's 'positive image' in the town.

The university's visibility was in some contrast to the garrison's unobtrusiveness. A disciplined professional army made less impact on the town as its own facilities improved. A 1950s plan to relocate to land further south was still

137 Four prospective students provide a photo opportunity for the concrete rafts and towers of Essex University in 1966.

being finalised in 2000, by which time the old Victorian garrison was approaching the status of a national heritage site. Meanwhile Hyderabad and Meeanee Barracks were updated, Sabraon Barracks were demolished, Roman Barracks built, and Goojerat Barracks rebuilt. Although recently re-equipped, the military hospital was closed in 1977 after a spat with central government over local proposals that it should be the stand-in for a new district hospital.

Among the specialist units in Colchester was the Stores and Clothing Research & Development Establishment devising and testing new army equipment. Perhaps the best known arm of the garrison to a generation of national servicemen was its Military Corrective Training Centre (popularly called the 'glasshouse'), housed in the set of Nissen huts once used by German prisoners of war. Graduates included the East End gangsters the Kray twins, though most of its short-term residents had only offended army discipline. The Nissen huts were replaced in 1988.

Undoubtedly the garrison's most visible gift to the town was the Colchester Tattoo, held in Castle Park and linked via the Colchester Community Fund to the town's annual Carnival which had been revived in 1951 as part of a Festival of Colchester, linked to the Festival of

138   Part of a Colchester Tattoo in Castle Park in the late 1970s.

Britain in the same year. The Community Fund, run by volunteers, was itself an outstanding and sustained fund-raiser. Over the decades the Tattoo became ever more ambitious until it was the largest in Britain, taking place over three nights in August, assembling massed army bands on a scale not seen elsewhere, even at the more famous Edinburgh Tattoo. Financial constraint and security problems, born of 'the troubles' in Northern Ireland, first made the Tattoo an irregular event, then moved it from Castle Park, then saw its demise in 1990, by which time Tattoo and Carnival had raised almost half a million pounds for charity. By 2000 the Carnival itself had ceased, victim of complex modern safety requirements.

As headquarters of Eastern District the garrison covered a large wedge of 5,000 acres to the south of the town. By 1990 it was on paper the town's main employer, home to 5,000 troops and their families, giving employment to 1,000 Colchester residents. By 2000 it was home to the Parachute Regiment and the helicopter-borne 16th Air Assault Brigade, and on the verge of its long-postponed £1 billion redevelopment, worth, by one estimate, £100 million a year to the local economy, scheduled to become in the 21st century the premier garrison in Britain. At the same date the 200-acre University of Essex was also expanding, had over 5,000 students and gave employment to a further 1,000 Colchester residents.

Employment

The immediate post-war years had been ones of full employment. Engineering now provided over 20 per cent of male employment in the town, excluding the military. A growing number of women workers reflected the growth of the clerical and administrative side of these businesses. The workforce at Paxman's, still the town's largest employer, fluctuated between 2,000 and 2,500 until 1980. The firm's financial position had been secured by becoming part of Ruston's of Lincoln, a key factor being the mutual respect of their managing director Victor Bone and Edward (Ted) Paxman, whose vee-form diesel engine was the basis of the Colchester firm's success. Still a significant exporter, Paxman's made engines and boilers in considerable numbers: for electricity generation; marine propulsion; oilfield exploration, including offshore platforms; and railway traction. For a while they had an important filtration section. Always a family firm, they now had members of the third generation of local families working for them. Though wage levels were not high and working conditions, particularly before the 1960s, were often basic, Paxman's was a big firm and a 'job for life' was preferable to uprooting your family to go to an equivalent firm in another part of Britain.

Wood's, led initially by the flamboyant Geoffrey Wood, in their expanding new site off Bergholt Road, refined the axial flow fan, becoming the largest exporter of industrial fans in the world. By 1960 the workforce had risen to 1,400, the firm selling more than 2,000 fans a year from its branded Xpelair window fan to giant industrial installations of all kinds. Export-led, the Colchester Lathe Company produced more than 3,000 lathes a year on a production line basis and now employed 600 or so staff, though this was to rise to 1,500 by 1970. Brackett's manufactured pumps and specialist water filtration equipment, notably for nuclear power stations, and employed about 250 staff.

More than 300 were employed by Betts, a London company of tube makers, who opened a Colchester factory in 1952; Bernard Mason's giant chemical paper, photocopying and office equipment empire on Cowdray Avenue employed at its peak 1,200 workers. Spottiswoode Ballantyne, the printers, employed 260 at their works at the Hythe, where the Moler works made 14 million industrial insulating bricks a year. Benham's, printers and owners of the main local newspapers, built large newspaper printing works at Sheepen Road, pioneering the web-offset process for newsprint.

These firms were but the stars in a broad firmament of male manufacturing industry which would also include the shipyards at Wivenhoe and Rowhedge usually employing almost 500. Other firms reflected the extent to which a Colchester workforce might travel for daily employment. In 1949, for example, the future Margaret Thatcher (then Roberts) settled in Cambridge Road, becoming secretary of the Colchester Young Conservatives while working as an industrial chemist at BX Plastics in Brantham.

Manufacturing industry also included the clothing factories which still employed more than 800, mostly female. The building industry (Hill's, Hutton's and Vaughan's figured

139 The green-field site of Wood's new factory complex, completed in time for the Second World War. Note the six parked cars and the steam train approaching Colchester's North Station.

prominently) usually employed about 1,250, a classic case in which firms or employees might come from a wider catchment area. There were more than 1,600 in transport: rail, road transport and on the buses (still before 1965 the main method of civilian travel). The 1951 Census records fewer than 2,000 'professional and technical' staff, both male and female. This compares with more than 2,500 (mostly male) clerks and (mostly female) typists, many working for the manufacturing firms already listed, while more than 1,000 women still worked in 'domestic service' compared with 744 shop assistants.

A marked characteristic of the pre-1960 era was the extent to which the family business still dominated the local scene, a characteristic, incidentally, still evident in the town's shops. In consequence perhaps 80 per cent of local employees served a boss whom they knew and who lived in the town. Family businesses ran flourishing sports and social clubs, their own pension schemes, their own works outings and Christmas parties, where the boss might look on benignly as standards began to slip.

This rather parochial situation was matched by a willingness to help one another. When,

140 The one that got away: the giant 'Post Office tower' under construction in 1969 in the heart of the Dutch Quarter, built despite local disapproval under Crown immunity.

after the war, Ted Paxman founded the Colchester Industries Association (where status hinged on the size of your workforce), he offered fellow businessmen export-dedicated diesel generators to supply their own electricity during the power cuts of the winter of 1951. Face-to-face business gave added importance to the local freemasons, Chamber of Commerce and Rotary Club. It was Colchester Rotary, not the town council, who came up with a worthy War Memorial proposal, the conversion of the run-down Provident Place into the Balkerne Gardens Trust, pioneering a range of private-communal facilities for the elderly which would be a model for the future, as life expectancy rose. Somewhat to their own surprise and greatly to the surprise of their sponsors, Rotary and the local churches raised

the £20,000 needed to gain funds from the Nuffield Foundation.

Such public spirit was in some contrast to the bureaucratic regimes of the public sector, which, with their national management structures, national rates of pay and multiple grades of appointment, became a major part of the Colchester employment scene. The Regional Hospital Board employed many hundreds, as did the nationalised utilities of gas and electricity. The Post Office headquarters and the telephone exchange in West Stockwell Street housed another thousand, until replaced by the re-named British Telecom's towerblock, built in 1969 under crown immunity against local opposition. It was, however, evidence of a further revolution: widespread local ownership of telephones with national and international direct dialling capacity. BT soon employed more than 2,000 staff in the town. A new hospital took rather longer to arrive, as the old one on Lexden Road acquired ever more temporary additions, each a monument to 20th-century architecture and National Health Service under-funding. The new district hospital, promised for 1966, was finally opened by the Queen in 1985.

Education was another public sector provision. Remarkably, it returned to partial borough care from 1963 until 1974. By this date some 17 new schools had been built in Colchester by the county council, providing a revolution in the range and quality of educational provision. Colchester's Royal Grammar School and the Girl's County High School, traditional single-sex grammar schools, were meanwhile securing, via the Eleven Plus exam, the pick of academic ability in the district. By the 1970s the Eleven Plus was under fire and comprehensive schooling was being urged. At two General Elections in 1974 it was a major talking point in the town and Colchester eventually devised its own substitute for the Eleven Plus. In 1977, when the Labour

141 1979 pickets outside the strike-torn gates of Ozalid, the former Mason's factory, soon to become the Cowdray Centre. One placard says: '20 per cent claim for 20 per cent inflation'.

government initiated legislation to phase out grammar schools, foot-dragging at County Hall and in Colchester Borough Council enabled the two schools to survive until the general election of 1979 brought the Conservative Party to power. Both schools ended the century scoring among the best 'A' Level and GCSE results in state schools in the country.

The Gilberd School, the town's only selective technical school, did not survive, reopening as a comprehensive school on a new site at High Woods in 1980. Small sixth forms at other secondary schools were closed when the Gilberd site on North Hill reopened as a Sixth Form College. It too was highly successful, vastly increasing the 'stay-on' rate in the town and achieving nationally impressive 'A' Level and university entrance results.

The town's other major educational institution was the Technical College, called from 1976 the Colchester Institute. It ended the war on North Hill, transferring to award-winning, purpose-built premises in Sheepen Road in 1954. Extended in many phases, its student numbers soared to more than 7,000, making it the largest educational establishment

in Essex by the 1980s, as the range of its technical and academic programme grew. From 1968 a separate Adult Education College developed at Greyfriars and during the 1990s most local secondary schools pursued special areas of excellence, if only to secure the funding it ensured. By 2000 Colchester was a high performer in academic league tables, with a wide range of educational provision.

Leisure

Some of that educational provision might be termed recreational, undertaken by the curious or the retired, as Colchester after 1960 reflected the nation's larger leisure opportunities. In the 1950s a good deal of outdoor team sport was played, but a widening interest in indoor sport lay behind the building of a lavish indoor swimming pool and sports centre. Appropriate to the age, the sports centre became Leisure World in 1990 with its own Jacuzzi, financed by the profits of the Culver Precinct development and run on a trading basis. Colchester United, the town's professional soccer team, jogged along in the lower divisions of the Football League, seeing its greatest glory as an FA Cup giant

142 Action during Colchester United's famous defeat of Leeds United in February 1971.

killer at its tiny Layer Road ground. In 1947-8 it became the first non-league team to reach the fifth round with a glamorous tie against Stanley Mathews and Blackpool, and in 1971 it impressed the football world by defeating Leeds United, arguably the best team in Europe at the time. Such days seem now to be over. After a short spell outside the league, the team has survived through generous sponsors and the hope of a new stadium and ground, which, after a host of false dawns, was on the brink of realisation by 2000.

In 1962 Colchester Zoo opened. Thanks to committed owners and widespread car ownership it became a considerable success. The Essex Naturalist Trust was locally strong. With 'Constable County' to the north and the picturesque Wivenhoe waterfront to the south, the district was also home to a number of important artists. In 1958 the Minories, at the top of East Hill, was opened as an art gallery and, despite financial vicissitudes, was poised for major expansion by 2000.

In 1972, even as cinema audiences plummeted, the Colchester Repertory Theatre, which had struggled along in the old Corn Exchange through the war and after, was re-launched as the Mercury Theatre, built for £260,000 with an Arts Council grant and some impressive local fund-raising. From day one it was deemed

a success both as a building and a theatrical experience. As a business venture it was more challenging and, after a sticky patch (and a fire) in the 1990s, it emerged as virtually council-owned and underwritten. There is little doubt that local pride played a big part in all this and, as aldermen were abolished, church-going declined and the gentry withdrew to the hills, leisure icons like the theatre's director, David Forder, or Dick Grahame, Colchester United's manager against Leeds, became the best-known names in town.

Throughout these years Colchester's age and Roman roots remained the unique selling point as tourism came to be seen as an important local industry. Signposts on new approach roads announced 'Welcome to Colchester: Britain's Oldest Recorded Town'; a Tourist Information Office was opened opposite the castle. Sometimes reluctantly, but ultimately generously, the council resourced the Castle Museum and Holly Trees and expanded into Trinity Church and Tymperleys clock museum. Very serious money, raised laboriously by subscription and grant, was expended on restoring and stabilising both the castle and the Roman wall. By 2000 the castle was a nationally-recognised, regional showpiece, while the Colchester Archaeological Trust had a strong local following.

Leisure enhanced the achievements of voluntary groups. Old hardy annuals like the Colchester Rose Show and the Co-op Day were joined by new ones such as the Fireswim for charity, costumed History Fayres and the Lions' duck race in the river. King Coel's Kittens were outstanding fund-raisers at carnivals, Guy Fawkes fireworks shows and Father Christmas street collections. Bodies with a long yesterday: Scouts, Guides, St John Ambulance, Meals on Wheels, the Talking Newspaper, the Citizens Advice Bureau, Relate, not to mention the town's many churches, were still active in 2000. The town twinned with Wetzlar, Avignon and Imola. The Colchester Operatic Society, St Botolph's Church, the music department at the Colchester Institute, the town's successful accordion orchestra and a range of marching bands completed the arts picture. In 1993 Colchester finally secured, in SGR Colchester, a commercial radio station. A remarkable achievement of the '80s and '90s was the establishment and continuous funding of the St Helena Hospice and Day Centre via an army of voluntary helpers. The new YMCA in Magdalen Street and the Night Shelter have been two responses to the growing problem of homelessness at the close of the 20th century.

In the 1980s D.I.Y. stores proliferated, even where the town council had opposed them; in the 1990s mobile phone masts suffered similar harassment. Permissiveness brought the town's first licensed 'sex shop'. Wider and louder leisure saw the High Street blossom with convenience food outlets as downtown neighbourhoods complained about late night revellers. By the year 2000 a new 'night economy' had been identified when mainly 'the young' took over the central streets, their exuberance recorded on close-circuit television. Town centre pubs, their deaths prematurely foretold in the 1960s, remained livelier than ever, though their clientele were younger.

Wider still and wider

In 1974, after years of national debate, local government reorganisation created the new Colchester District Council: 60 councillors instead of 36, responsible for a population of 130,000, including 35 villages in Lexden and Winstree, Tiptree garden suburb, Wivenhoe at the river and Mersea over the water. It might have been otherwise. For a while it had been discussed whether to incorporate the town into Suffolk. Instead, Colchester now stretched as far as the eye could see. Two sets of officers had to be merged without offence, a difficult undertaking given their widely differing experience. The same might be said of rural councillors with their far smaller electorates. For a while the rural Conservatives were at war with their urban colleagues. The initiative was taken by the town clerk and his senior officers, a procedure that would accelerate over the next 30 years.

The political balance changed too. The Conservatives with their rural phalanx could and did control the council for a decade. Labour faced lifetime minority status. Party lines hardened. The winners took all the chairs and Labour boycotted the mayoralty, as instructions came down from party headquarters in London. Groups sat in blocks, drank tea in blocks, met in blocks before a committee. And, before the committee, there was the officer briefing.

In this confrontational world the room for manoeuvre was shrinking. County Hall and central government controlled the purse. After 1980 the Thatcher government systematically tied local government hands over spending aims and ceilings. Little changed thereafter, apart from the coming and going of the 'poll tax'. Rates had been found wanting, but were not replaced. One half of Colchester's council houses had been sold by 2000, but new ones could only be built via housing associations. The buses were privatised. In fact, they had lost money at a spectacular rate. In 1990 the

143 Senior Paxman staff discuss with senior Admiralty staff the merits of the highly successful 5,000 b.h.p. Valenta engine seen here in mock-up.

borough were glad to sell the lot for £1 plus £750,000 accumulated debts.

The political victor of this period was the Liberal Democrat Party, newly formed, which came to dominate the historic town and secure control of the district council. They also secured the Parliamentary seat with Bob Russell, the town's first genuinely local member for almost 150 years, after Sir Antony Buck, Conservative, had held the seat for almost 32 years. Viewed from 2000 the new district council had been, for Colchester, a success. The town maintained its historical continuity, its traditions and its town hall, while absorbing a wider area. This was less popular in the absorbed areas of Wivenhoe and Tiptree, who elected their own 'Residents Association' councillors.

The real problem lay in the continued stranglehold of Westminster and the new 'Cabinet' structure of government, concentrating power in a collective of five. This left elected councillors with less to do, and it became harder to find volunteers willing to stand. Colchester began the 21st century with the Cabinet posts shared between all three parties. Who, then, formed the opposition – the other councillors? And did it matter, when the officers ran the council anyway? This was the unspoken epitaph to the Millennium.

Throughout this uneasy *fin de siècle* Colchester continued to expand. Most growth still took place in the historic borough, though Stanway had now been effectively absorbed. Here the large Tollgate Centre provided one of several 'out-of-town' retail centres, source of an alleged threat to town-centre shopping. The fact is Colchester appeared to have room for both. To the north the borough-owned High Woods (once King's Wood) progressed towards its targeted 3,500 houses, alongside the newly designated High Woods Country Park. Close by was the expanding Severall's Business Park: a success story as Colchester had sought, over the previous 20 years, to entice new industry to the town, given the decline in manufacturing. In Colchester that decline really began in the 1980s: a decade in which, ironically, six Queen's Awards for Industry were won by local firms.

First to go were the old clothing factories, defeated, essentially, by cheap Far Eastern labour. The Colchester Lathe Company suffered a similar fate as Far Eastern companies bought its lathes and proceeded to copy them. The workforce shrank. The Moler Works, though fully profitable, were purchased by rivals who relocated production to France. Mason's did not survive Bernard Mason's departure, running through several amalgamations (and far more managing directors), until it rose from its own ashes as the Cowdray Centre, a home for small businesses. Here Dynapert, world leaders in electronic components, employed 400 until gobbled up by rivals.

Paxman's and Wood's had earlier migrated from family ownership to the giant G.E.C. combine. In Paxman's case this led to the closure of some departments. Nevertheless, they continued to produce new engines, notably for the Royal Navy and railways the world over, including high-speed trains in Australia and the

U.K. In 1973 and 1987 Paxman engineers twice broke the world speed record for diesel-hauled passenger trains on Intercity routes. Smaller order books and the inflation of the 1980s led to bitter trade disputes, as the firm progressively reduced its workforce. Yet the smaller company still designed and produced another world-class engine, the VP185, in the 1990s.

Wood's, by contrast, were growing in size as the clean and quiet air they supplied was in international demand. The break up of the G.E.C. empire saw Paxman's sold to a French company who sold them to old rivals, MAN, B & W of Germany. The century ended with hopes that this would bring a bright future. Instead, Paxman's effectively closed, its engine manufacture moved to Stockport. With a trimmed workforce, Wood's found a future tied to Global Air Movements who were soon considering the viability of the Braiswick site. After dramatic job losses, the Lathe Company was moved from Colchester to Yorkshire. Brackett's lived on, tied to Hawker Siddeley; Courtauld's acquired Betts. The 260-year-old printers, Spottiswoode's, closed. These blows to old Colchester firms not only demonstrated that footloose industries can run away, but that globalisation has local consequences.

The 1981 and 2001 censuses record a 28 per cent fall in those engaged locally in manufacturing industry against a 182 per cent rise in 'service' occupations: finance, retail, wholesale and hospitality. Manufacturing was always a mainly male activity and most forms of servicing, female. The increase in the latter coincided with a revolution in the local workforce as the number of employed women came to equal that of men, though in the case of women, as with the new jobs, many were part-time.

Some work came with newcomers. The removal of the Middleborough livestock market enabled Colchester to provide a home for Royal London Insurance who relocated

from London, sponsored local football and the arts, and had their own 'castle' built in 1982 wherein to employ their staff of 1,200. Philips Business briefly camped at North Station. By 2000 both these giants had gone and Colchester had its first telephone 'call centre' employing 700 staff. The top ten employers in 2000 were mostly institutions, one manufacturer and several finance bodies. The Army, the Co-op, the local Health Care Trust and the University headed the list, though the 1990s had seen serious downsizing in a public sector more open to market forces. The town's average wage was low. Many of the new workplaces were small, many ephemeral, many were old ones transformed, full of 'management speak', where heads of department were called 'pathway leaders'. Movements into and out of the town for work became yet more important.

Did Colchester in consequence face an identity crisis? Old certainties had truly gone: Paxman's, the Carnival, the cosy borough council. The Hythe had closed as a port. The shift of the Middleborough livestock market and of tractor sales on Hythe Hill finally dispelled any 'feel' that this was an agricultural town. Care in the Community had closed both Severall's and Turner Village: in 2000 they awaited so-called 'brown field' development, a fate already suffered by Paxman's foundry tip.

Colchester no longer lay in a backwater. A dual-carriageway A12 had given the Bypass a bypass and links with Felixstowe Docks; a dualled A120 would link with the expanding Stansted airport, though the northern and eastern arms of the 1962 ring road were still not built. 'Gridlock' and 'infrastructure' were familiar words in the 1990s. The 'school run' now caused as much chaos as the 'rush hour'. On-street parking was a way of life. One-third of local households had two or more cars; a quarter had one inhabitant. The town must have been full of empty bedrooms. MORI polls in

144 This 1988 view of Balkerne Hill shows how the incomplete inner ring-road has bred a new urban geography. Office blocks curve round the Maldon Road Roundabout; the Royal London and Anglia Water complexes (both empty by 2000) dominate the bottom of the hill; and the St Mary's Car Park and Mercury Theatre align themselves with the dual carriageway. This in turn displays the Roman Wall as it has not been seen for 2000 years.

1992 and 1996 showed general satisfaction with living in Colchester. Population had grown more by in-migration than by reproduction. By 2001 there were more over 60s than under 15s in the town.

There is a view that all southern England is now an interlocked 'urbanised' web: that distinctions between town and country only exist in our heads. The variety of modern life gives us many allegiances. Living in suburbs in unprecedented comfort, our nuclear family, our partner, our passion for gardening, our Internet chatroom can fill our horizon. Stars of television can be more real (and better known) than the mayor of Colchester, Coronation Street more meaningful than High Street. Are we now citizens of Britain, Colchester or Estuary England? The answer, of course, is all three. Colchester residents shop at Lakeside, Thurrock, roam the M25 and holiday in Spain. The local press might report on Colchester United even when Manchester United rules in many school playgrounds.

But Colchester is not yet a housing estate off the A12. With a central shopping centre, much of it pedestrianised, a range of local papers, an elected district council, a professional football club and its own M.P., Colchester still has much that proclaims it is a town, that sustains the image, if not the reality, of an old self-governing marketplace, surrounded by open countryside, on a river, on a hill. The bin bags are collected, flowers grow in Castle Park, daffodils explode along the verges, a mayor sits in the town hall and people notice if he or she attends a local event. The past is also present. Citizens are proud of their museum in their castle, in their park. The competition to be a tourist guide is intense. The King's Wood can still be seen from North Hill, a Roman road which, like the castle, has changed a bit since King John was here. Georgian houses, Edwardian pubs, civic and commercial publicists all feel the need to proclaim Colchester's long history.

And, if you are really lucky, residents buy books about the history of the town.

Concise Bibliography

Benham, Hervey, *Essex at War* (1946)

Benham, W.G. (trans.), *The Red Paper Book of Colchester* (1902), *The Colchester Oath Book* (1907)

Britnell, R.H., *Growth and Decline in Colchester 1300-1525* (1986)

Brown, A.F.J., *Colchester in the 18th Century* (1969)

Brown, A.F.J., *Colchester 1815-1914* (1980)

Clarke, Palliser and Daunton (eds.), *The Cambridge Urban History of Britain* [3 vols.] (2000)

Cooper, Janet (ed.), *Victoria County History of Essex, Volume 9*

Clarke, David T.D. and Joan Clarke, *Camulodunum* (1971)

Clarke, David T.D., *The Siege of Colchester 1648* (1974)

Cockerill, Chloe and Daphne Woodward, *The Siege of Colchester* (1979)

Crummy, Philip, *City of Victory* (1997)

Crummy, Philip, *Aspects of Anglo-Saxon and Norman Colchester* (1981)

Cunliffe, Barry, *The Ancient Celts* (1997)

Dunnett, Rosalind, *The Trinovantes* (1975)

Higgs, Laquita, *Godliness and Governance in Tudor Colchester* (1998)

Holland, M., and Cooper, J. [eds.], *Essex Harvest* (2003)

Hull, M.R., *Roman Colchester* (1958)

Martin, Geoffrey, *The Story of Colchester from Roman times to the Present Day* (1959)

Moote, Lloyd and Dorothy, *The Great Plague: the story of London's most deadly year* (2004)

Morant, Philip, *The History and Antiquities of the Most Ancient Town and Borough of Colchester* (1748)

Phillips, Andrew, *Ten Men and Colchester* (1985)

Phillips, Andrew, *Colchester 1940-1990: a changing town* (1996)

Sealey, Paul R., *The Boudican Revolt against Rome* (1997)

Stephenson, David, *The Book of Colchester* (1978)

Wacher, John, *The Towns of Roman Britain* (2nd edn. 1986)

Walter, John, *Understanding Popular Violence in the English Revolution: the Colchester Plunderers* (1999)

OTHER SOURCES

The Colchester Archaeologist 1987–present

Essex Archaeology & History (3rd Series) 1961–present

Essex County Standard 1831–present

Evening Gazette 1970–present

The 'Colchester Recalled' Oral History Collection

Index

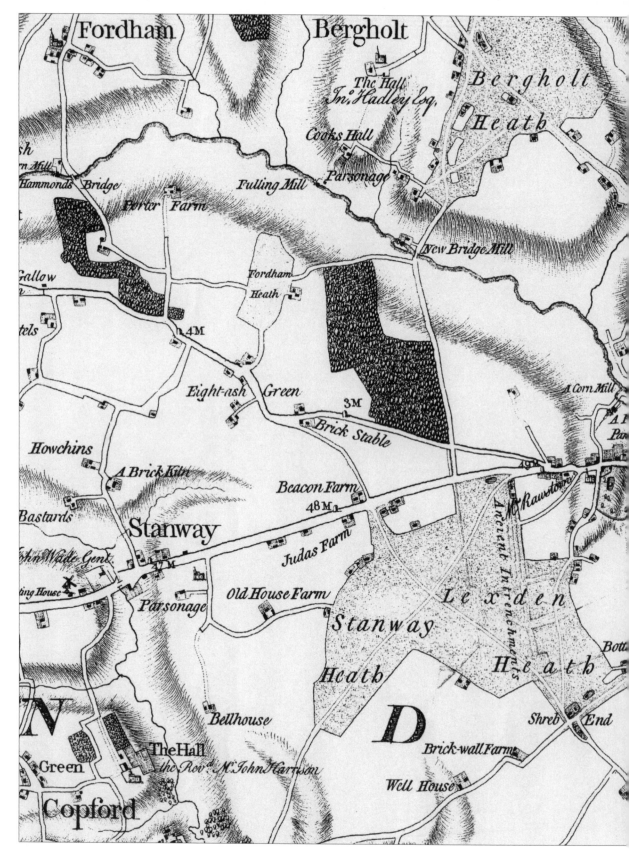

Chapman and André Map of 1777